Twayne's United States Authors Series

EDITOR OF THIS VOLUME

David L. Nordloh

Indiana University

Mary Hallock Foote

TUSAS 369

Mary Hallock Foote

MARY HALLOCK FOOTE

By LEE ANN JOHNSON

TWAYNE PUBLISHERS

A DIVISION OF G. K. HALL & CO., BOSTON

Published in 1980 by Twayne Publishers,
A Division of G. K. Hall & Co.
All Rights Reserved

Printed on permanent/durable acid-free paper and bound
in the United States of America

First Printing

Library of Congress Cataloging in Publication Data

Johnson, Lee Ann.
Mary Hallock Foote.

(Twayne's United States authors series ; TUSAS 369)
Bibliography: p. 172-76
Includes index.
1. Foote, Mary Hallock, 1847-1938.   2.   Authors,
American—19th century—Biography
PS1688.J6   813'.4 [B]   79-24294
ISBN 0-8057-7231-6

In memory of my father,
L. Robert Loving, Jr.

Lay this Laurel on the One
Too intrinsic for Renown-
Laurel—vail your deathless tree—
Him you chasten, that is He!

Emily Dickinson

Contents

About the Author

Lee Ann Johnson was educated at the University of Texas, where she received her B.A. in 1967. She received her M.A. and Ph.D. from the University of California, Los Angeles, where she specialized in nineteenth-century American literature. Dr. Johnson has taught at Michigan State University, lectured at the School of International Studies in Tokyo, and was a Fulbright-Hays Lecturer at the University of Seville, Spain, during 1975-76. Professor Johnson has published in *Nineteenth-Century Fiction, Twentieth Century Literature, Studies in Philology, Arizona Quarterly,* and several other scholarly journals. She is presently a law student at the University of California, Berkeley.

Preface

Though overlooked by literary and cultural historians until recently, Mary Hallock Foote occupied a noteworthy position in American letters for more than four decades. Between 1880 and 1925 she published twelve novels and four volumes of short stories, wrote a distinguished autobiography, and authored numerous uncollected tales and sketches. What makes this productivity especially impressive is that she did not dedicate herself exclusively to literature. While to the nineteenth-century reading public she was best known as a literary interpreter of the West, she enjoyed equal fame in art and publishing circles as the leading woman illustrator of her day. Viewed from a twentieth-century perspective, Foote's combined talents as an author-illustrator place her in a very select group whose union of graphic and verbal skills represents a special genius.

Her achievements, particularly in literature, are best analyzed within their biographical context, for Mary Hallock Foote was a woman driven by the need to give form, through art, to her inner life. Her characters frequently reflect the whole of her personality, both conscious and unconscious; and her fiction is often most compelling when it transforms material rooted deeply in her own experience. In this last respect she was favored, as an author and illustrator, with richly varied experiences on which to draw.

Born in 1847 to a Quaker farming family in the Hudson River valley, Mary Hallock Foote was extremely attached to rural homelife. With marriage in 1876, however, came the dilemma of "transplantation," for her husband's career as a mining engineer dictated residence in the Far West. The next twenty years brought a seemingly endless series of moves which strongly tested her capacity to adapt to new surroundings. Yet she withstood the hardships of mining camp life in Colorado, Idaho, and California, raising three children and converting the frontier experiences into artistic and literary capital. Her illustrations of the West were recognized by her contemporaries as remarkable, while several of her mining camp novels became modest bestsellers. Fame proved transitory, however, for Mary Hallock Foote. In the years following 1919, when she ceased to publish, her achievements receded from the public memory, and she passed the final years of her life in comparative obscurity.

Of those who subsequently rediscovered Foote, none has been more influential than Wallace Stegner and Rodman Paul. The first to anthologize one of Foote's short stories, Stegner observed in 1958, "To the shrinking list of the enduring and worthy one would like to add the name of Mary Hallock Foote, both writer and illustrator."[1] Perceiving her life to be an intriguing model of the values and manners of her era, Stegner used Foote as the inspiration for his Pulitzer-Prize winning novel *Angle of Repose*, which appeared in 1971. The following year marked the publication of Paul's superb edition of *A Victorian Gentlewoman in the Far West: The Reminiscences of Mary Hallock Foote*, the fascinating retrospective Foote wrote during the early 1920s.

With the *Reminiscences* available, the time is propitious for a full-length consideration of Mary Hallock Foote's achievements. My purpose in writing this critical biography is to place Foote within her milieu, to bring to light the hidden excellence of her work, and to provide a starting point for contemporary appraisals of her contribution to American letters. While I have striven for a balanced presentation, I have not hesitated, when page limitations made it necessary, to be selective. Few of Foote's illustrations have been singled out for discussion, several of her uncollected prose pieces are not analyzed, and her juvenile fiction has been considered only when it illumines a phase of her artistic or emotional development.

For their gracious cooperation with this project I wish to thank the granddaughters of Mary Hallock Foote—Janet Foote Micoleau, Marian Foote Conway, Evelyn Foote Gardiner, Sarah Swift, and Agnes Swift. Special thanks are also due to Rosamond Gilder, donor of the Foote-Gilder correspondence, and to Patricia J. Palmer and Michelle C. Leiser, Manuscripts Division of the Stanford University Library, whose familiarity with the Foote materials proved invaluable. To Robert P. Falk, Velma B. Richmond, Glenda J. McGee, and Diane A. Ward—each of whom read this manuscript in its early stages—I am particularly grateful; their counsel resulted in sounder thought and clearer expression throughout. And to Don, who urged this study through to completion, I owe the greatest debt of all.

LEE ANN JOHNSON

Walnut Creek, California

Chronology

1847 Mary Anna Hallock born November 19 on a farm near Milton, New York; youngest of four children of Nathaniel and Ann Burling Hallock, Quakers.

1864 Begins three years of studies at the Cooper Institute School of Design for Women in New York City. Studies illustration under William James Linton. Begins lifelong friendship with Helena de Kay, who later marries Richard Watson Gilder.

1867 Publishes four black-and-white drawings in A. D. Richardson's *Beyond the Mississippi*, marking her debut as a professional illustrator.

1873 Meets Arthur De Wint Foote, of a distinguished family from Guilford, Connecticut.

1875 Initiates her literary career with "The Picture in the Fire-place Bedroom." Meets Longfellow and Howells, gaining entrée to Boston's select circle of authors and artists.

1876 Marries Arthur Foote. Moves to New Almaden, California, where Arthur works as a mining engineer.

1877 Illustrates Longfellow's *The Skeleton in Armor* and Hawthorne's *The Scarlet Letter*. After birth of son, Arthur Burling, moves to Santa Cruz, California, to be near Arthur's new assignment.

1878 Returns to Milton while Arthur pursues field engineering. Her prose first appears in *Scribner's Monthly*.

1879 Makes summer-long visit to Arthur in Leadville, Colorado.

1880 Moves to Leadville; in September, the Footes return to Milton.

1881 Accompanies Arthur on business trip to Mexico.

1882 Remains in Milton while Arthur begins Idaho irrigation venture. Birth of daughter, Elizabeth ("Betty").

1883 Publishes *The Led-Horse Claim*, her first novel.

1884   Moves to Boise, Idaho, to rejoin Arthur.

1886   *John Bodewin's Testimony.* Birth of daughter, Agnes.

1889   "Pictures of the Far West" (illustrations). *The Last Assembly Ball.*

1892   *The Chosen Valley.*

1893   Selected as an Art Juror for the Columbian Exposition (Chicago World's Fair).

1894   *Coeur d'Alene. In Exile, and Other Stories.*

1895   *The Cup of Trembling, and Other Stories.* Moves to Grass Valley, California, where Arthur has accepted a mining position.

1899   *The Little Fig-Tree Stories.*

1900   *The Prodigal.*

1902   *The Desert and the Sown.*

1903   *A Touch of Sun and Other Stories.*

1904   Death of Agnes.

1910   *The Royal Americans.*

1912   *A Picked Company.*

1915   *The Valley Road.*

1917   *Edith Bonham.*

1919   *The Ground-Swell.*

1922   Begins *Reminiscences,* published posthumously in 1972.

1932   Moves with Arthur to Hingham, Massachusetts, to live with Betty.

1933   Death of Arthur, August 24.

1938   Dies June 25.

CHAPTER 1

The Quaker Artist

IN the third decade of the twentieth century, nearly eighty years after her birth, Mary Hallock Foote began an endeavor urged by her family—the recording of the experiences which had made hers such a remarkable life. For many years her autobiography, in variant manuscript versions, remained unpublished, its insights treasured by her descendants. Regardless of the draft read, Foote's reminiscences usually began with a passage emphasizing her Quaker origins:

> When the English colonists of the year 1640 took the westward ocean trail, among them was a dissenting minister, the Reverend Peter Hallock, who settled, with members of his flock, on an edge of Long Island afterwards called Hallock Neck. They found a continent that was all frontier, and as they pushed back that curtain of primeval forests, they set up barriers of their own of racial prejudice and religious beliefs that lasted longer than Nature's walls.
> The Reverend Peter had a grandson, John Hallock, who shocked his family by marrying a Quaker girl. He was "disinherited," legend says, which naturally confirmed his choice and made Quakers of his line. John is our ancestor on the Hallock side. On three other sides of our "house," the Townsends, Hulls, and Burlings, there also was one wretched son who would not fight, even Indians, nor pray in the words of the Preacher, but in silence, alone with the Inner Spirit which he claimed was God. It was more likely the devil, his kindred said, and they cut him off, to start a branch of his own. In each of these dissenting breeds we are the Quaker branch that went too far and was left on a frontier of its own.[1]

The frontier mentality, the quiet strength born of isolated circumstances, was to prove among the most valuable legacies of Foote's parentage. When, as a wife and mother, she faced unusual hardships in the Far West, she was sustained by the resourcefulness which had been a vital necessity from earliest childhood. Though hers was not a Quaker household in the West, she retained throughout her life the gentle demeanor yet firm resolve which characterized her ancestors.

I Rural Beginnings

Born November 19, 1847, on a sidehill farm in Ulster County, New York, Mary Anna Hallock was raised in a rural setting both picturesque and remote. The family homestead, situated on an original tract of land secured by Mary's paternal great grand-father from Queen Anne, lay half a mile west of the Hudson River. While the home was within walking distance of the little village of Milton, communication with the larger towns to the south was incommodious, generally involving travel by hack four miles northward to New Paltz landing, then by ferry eastward to Poughkeepsie, and from there a boat trip down the Hudson. As a rule, the Hallocks did not mingle with their worldly neighbors; to the local villagers the retiring family was known derisively as the "Quaker Hallocks" and their vicinity dubbed "Hallock Hallow."[2] Nor did they commune with other New York Quakers, for a strong antislavery position adopted by Mary's paternal uncle had resulted in the exclusion of the "Hicksite" Hallocks from the New York Meeting and their consequent withdrawal into the ranks of family. Thus from an early age "Molly," as she was called by family, came to rely chiefly upon the companionship of her three older siblings—Philadelphia, Tom, and Bessie—and upon her own resources.

The silent fortitude of the Hallock family was embodied in Mary's mother, Ann Burling Hallock, who possessed "the unconscious loveliness of that typical New York gentlewoman of the Quaker breed, English not Dutch; not a society woman in the least,—all that would be impossible to a descendant of 'Friends,' but an exquisite gentlewoman unspotted from the world." Quiet and retiring, Mrs. Hallock exerted a remarkable influence on her family. "[S]aying little, comprehending everything, surprised at nothing,"[3] she exacted strict obedience and won unquestioning devotion. From her mother Mary inherited her refined instinct, unpretentious manner, and firm belief that one's behavior should befit her station in life.

Mrs. Hallock's reserve complemented the energy of her husband, who "belonged to the last of his breed of thinking and

reading American farmers." Nathaniel Hallock's strong interest
in the world of letters deeply influenced Mary. On days when
she was permitted to accompany him on rounds of the farm, she
delighted in his habit of quoting liberally from favorite authors,
and she recalled one such occasion long afterwards:

. . . I remember a morning when my winter coat was put on before
breakfast to go with father—a great privilege—to the upper barn along
the icy lanes in March, to see him feed cut-turnips to the yearling
lambs. The sun just risen at our backs made our shadows all legs
streaking ahead of us; his seemed to end over in the next field, and he
pointed to it and quoted from one of his old classics (Thomson's *Seasons*
very likely), "Prepost'rous sight! the legs without the man." I missed
the context, but that word "prepost'rous" I never forgot—nor the low
light so different from sunset streaming across the glistening fields; nor
the faces of the lambs crowding about my father's knees as he waded
through their warm, bleating bodies to the barn.[4]

Mary looked forward to the evenings when her father would
read aloud to the family from a variety of materials, ranging from
contemporary poetry to congressional debates and editorials
published in the *New York Tribune.* His library was stocked with
the most recent issues of the *Atlantic Monthly* and *Harper's
Weekly,* and with numerous volumes by Tennyson, Scott, Burns,
Cowper, and Pope. Hallock's predilection for the Victorians, and
especially for their poetry, shaped the course of his daughter's
early reading. By the age of sixteen she had read narrowly but
deeply, immersing herself in Browning, Rossetti, and Tennyson.
The last became the author upon whom she most frequently
drew for inspiration in her own writing, the author whom she
"read at all ages."

If Mary's father was interested in literature and public affairs,
her widowed Aunt Sarah was equally so. An active member of
the New York Anti-Slavery Society, she invited to the Hallock
homestead such famous figures of the period as Frederick
Douglass, Susan B. Anthony, and Ernestine L. Rose. Thus, despite
the family's self-imposed isolation, Mary was exposed to many of
the momentous issues stirring the United States during the 1850s.
As she later observed in her *Reminiscences,* "I have always
regarded this phantasmagoria of idealists and propagandists and
militant cranks and dreamers as one of the great opportunities of
our youth. . . . For they were brilliant talkers; all the villages in

the valley of the Hudson and Mohawk put together could not have furnished such conversation as we heard without stirring from our firesides."[5]

Mary began her formal education in a private Quaker school on the family property. There she excelled in mathematics and read for the first time such Quaker classics as Whittier's "Barclay of Ury" and Hawthorne's "The Gentle Boy," both of which she termed "unforgettable."[6] By the time she entered Poughkeepsie Female Collegiate Seminary for her high-school years, her artistic inclination had become pronounced. She began taking drawing classes at the seminary, while at home she practiced her art by using Bessie, six years her senior, as model. The relationship between the budding artist and her supportive elder sibling developed into a lifelong intimacy; for Molly, Bessie would always be "half mother as well as sister"—"half angel."

Had it not been for Bessie, and for the generous intervention of Tom's wife, Sarah Walter Hallock, Mary would have concluded her schooling with the seminary, as was traditional for a young lady of the period. But both women recognized Mary's abilities and succeeded in convincing the Hallocks that she should seek further training in art. After considerable discussion, it was arranged that Mary would live with Sarah's family in Brooklyn Heights in order to attend the Women's School of Design at Cooper Union.[7] In the fall of 1864, just before she turned seventeen, Mary left the reassuringly familiar Hudson River countryside for the excitement and uncertainty of life in New York City.

II *Artistic Awakening*

Like her older contemporary Henry David Thoreau, who claimed he had been "born in the most favorable spot on earth— and just in the nick of time, too," Mary Hallock Foote considered herself fortunate to come of age on the east coast at the time and place most favorable to the development of her talents. The Cooper Union had been in existence only seven years when she sought admission. Its School of Design was, as one of Mary's classmates later observed, "the only place, at that time, where anything approaching an art education could be had for a girl."[8] The Union had been envisioned by its founder, Peter Cooper, as

a "free school, library, and debating club for artisans and women
otherwise precluded from furthering their skills in design,
engineering, and public speaking."[9] The scene of a celebrated
address by Abraham Lincoln in 1860, the school also attracted
lecturers of such repute as Mark Twain and Bertrand Russell.

Mary embraced her new opportunities with youthful
exuberance. In her daily two-mile commute from the Walter
home to Cooper Union she must have made a small but striking
figure: according to one account, her blue eyes and light brown
hair were complemented by "such white skin and such brilliant
color in her cheeks that she often had to wear a veil because men
thought that she was painted." Many years later one of her
classmates, Helena de Kay Gilder, recalled her early impressions
of Mary:

> It was there [at Cooper Union] that I first saw her—very youthful in
> figure, delicate and yet full of vigor. She rode well. . . . She skated on
> her little feet like a swallow flying, and danced with the same grace and
> lightness. She could outskate and outdance us all.
> Besides these untaught arts she had the serious ones of woman's life
> . . . and had the dainty precision which has always seemed to me the
> mark of a true lady.[10]

With Helena—daughter of a prominent New York family and
future wife of Richard Watson Gilder, the poet and editor of
Century Illustrated Monthly Magazine—Mary began what was to
become the most significant friendship of her life. For more than
forty years—until Helena's death—the shy Quaker and the New
York society figure remained united through an extensive and
brilliant correspondence which reconciled the greatly dissimilar
life-styles and vast geographical distance which sought to
separate them. In print, evidence of their mutual admiration—
and of their considerable literary abilities—survives in Helena's
laudatory 1894 essay on Foote, and in *Edith Bonham* (1917),
Mary's novelistic tribute to her best friend.

During her three years at Cooper, Mary became whole-
heartedly involved in the social activities that city and school life
afforded. "New York was the world to me," she later declared;
"I was too happy to be serious about anything, and too mixed up
learning to know myself and so many other things. Art never was
to me, nor ever could be, the whole of life."[11] Yet despite all the

competing attractions, she worked diligently at her studies and determined black-and-white commercial illustration to be the proper field for her talents.

From William Rimmer and William J. Linton—the two men whom she later credited as the greatest influences on her work[12]—she learned the techniques of woodcut illustration, a branch of art which attracted few amateurs because of its difficulty. She was taught to draw directly on the wood block rather than to use the easier but less satisfactory procedure of drawing on thin paper and then tracing the reverse image on wood. The difficulty of her task was increased when, in order to assure a more faithful product, she chose to use pencil rather than pen and ink. To make her drawing, she had to prepare the surface of the block, usually cut from 7/8-inch boxwood, with powdered bath-brick or chinese wash. Then, using the direct black-line method, she would pencil in her sketch, which would appear as a dark line against a white background. The block would be forwarded to an engraver, who would excise the white and engrave the black lines on each of their sides. The image Mary had drawn would thus appear in relief, and, when inked, would produce her drawing upon a white page.

Though she found the process difficult, Mary was not easily defeated. As she confided to Helena,

I feel the lack of technical knowledge, especially on these big blocks. I don't know how to work effectively and my sketches are always better than my blocks. I am afraid I shall have to exile myself for a couple of months next winter and try to acquire a little of that free and yet precise way of working which makes the men's work so much more successful than ours.[13]

Determinedly, she sought instruction from John H. E. Whitney and Charles H. Burt, both of New York City, and spent a term studying under Samuel Frost Johnson. By late 1867, when she returned to her family, her efforts had been rewarded with her first professional commission. Prophetically, her inaugural assignment was for illustrations of the West. Molly Hallock, who as Mary Hallock Foote would achieve her greatest reputation as a literary interpreter of the Far West, began her career with four black-and-white drawings for A. D. Richardson's *Beyond the Mississippi*, published in 1867 when she was twenty. Once launched, her career gave no pause: "I was in high spirits . . .

considerably puffed up, after my drawings began to sell, with that pride of independence which was a new thing to daughters of that period."[14]

She was on her way to becoming, as W. J. Linton would later acknowledge, "the best of our designers on the wood"; and she was wise enough to recognize that her early success was partially attributable to timing. Freeing itself from the restraint of the second-rate, woodcut illustration in America was experiencing a radical transformation. During the 1870s, 1880s, and 1890s it entered what critics have called its golden age; the productions of this period were never surpassed, though they were supplanted by the more efficient photo-engraving process in the twentieth century. At the beginning of this heyday the art editors of *Scribner's Monthly* were, as one observer commented, "the first in America to make the best their aim."[15] Fortunately for Mary, Richard Watson Gilder—whom she met during her Cooper days and who married her best friend, Helena—was by 1870 the de facto editor of that magazine. Recognizing his friend's superior abilities, he promoted her as one of *Scribner's* most accomplished illustrators. A survey of issues between 1870 and 1874 reveals that Mary's work soon appeared with the same frequency as that of such acknowledged artists as Edwin Austin Abbey and Joseph Pennell.[16] Moreover, she was early given the opportunity to illustrate the works of such prominent authors of the period as Bret Harte, Constance Fenimore Woolson, and Adeline Trafton.

Through her mentor W. J. Linton—whose contacts included A. V. S. Anthony, head of the art department of Fields, Osgood & Company (later Houghton Mifflin)—Mary was commissioned to do a Fields giftbook which sent her career into ascendancy. Her illustrations for Henry Wadsworth Longfellow's *The Hanging of the Crane*, completed in 1874, were received by the author and publishers with genuine pleasure. From Milton, Mary wrote a facetious letter to Helena detailing her triumph:

Mr. A. says that Mr. Longfellow was as much pleased as he was *surprised* when he found they were made by a young lady! Complimentary to young women in general—don't you think so? What is the use of doing anything more than is expected of "young ladies"! Mr. Longfellow asked Mr. Anthony if I was "handsome and accomplished" and how *old* I was. These, you see, are the important questions.[17]

Longfellow apparently found the answers to his liking, for early
in 1875 Mary was summoned to Boston for her artistic debut.
Invited to dine with Longfellow and his distinguished friends—
Oliver Wendell Holmes, James Russell Lowell, and William Dean
Howells among them—she termed the event "the surprise of my
life." In her autobiography she recalled modestly, "Everyone
knows how generous they were, those makers of American
literature, to all the young pilgrims who worshipped at their
shrines. You went to Boston for the accolade and your shoulders
tingled ever after."[18]

The success of the Longfellow giftbook brought Mary
favorable reviews and new commissions. Howells observed of
the *Crane* drawings,

> It is in the conception as well as the execution of her work that Miss
> Hallock will delight the appreciative reader. She has exactly expressed
> in her pictures the general and impersonal sense of the poem; . . .
> Every picture indeed is suffused with the light of a quick and refined
> sympathy; and this is reinforced by a skillful pencil which has, so far as
> we can observe, no unpleasant tricks or mannerisms.[19]

George Parsons Lathrop averred that the drawings established
her reputation upon a "solid foundation," while John Greenleaf
Whittier's favorable impression of her work led to the collaboration of the young Quaker from New York with New England's
famous Quaker poet on an edition of *Hazel-Blossoms* (1875),
followed by *Mabel Martin* (1876). The latter poem, an idyll of
simple rural life, was especially suited to Mary's interest and
talent, and the result pleased Whittier. "Never was there a
prettier book than '*Mabel Martin!*' " he enthused. "If it does not
sell well, it surely cannot be the fault of the publishers and
artists." Whittier asked to meet his principal artist, and the
occasion was later described by Anthony:

> . . . Mr. Whittier, for whose "Mabel Martin" Mrs. Foote had made
> some drawings, came to my house, to see her.
>   The little lady sat at his feet, on a "cricket"—I distinctly recall the
> Quaker kerchief she had about her neck—and she talked just as Mrs.
> Hopper [one of Mary's friends] said she would—
>   Howells, Aldrich and some others were there, but the little lady was
> the bright particular star.[20]

Judging from the laudatory reviews of Mary's early illustrations, hers was an art both fresh and accomplished, grounded on no particular school. Her precision was notable, as was her ability to capture subjects as varied as western drovers and eastern landscapes. But there was general agreement that rural scenes and feminine character studies constituted her particular genius. One cover for *Hearth and Home,* "On the Ice," perfectly captures the beauty and gaiety of millpond skating. Also noteworthy is a group of her early drawings—pencil sketches and studies of Milton life which she sold to Anthony—which were exhibited at Osgood & Company in 1876. Lathrop spoke of these pieces as treating "landscape and figure alike with an accuracy, a spiritualness, and a shaping skill which would be remarkable anywhere, and are especially rare in America." Helena Gilder also singled out several of these drawings for praise in her later published tribute to Foote. Although many items of this particular collection were never published, a few are to be found in an 1878 *Scribner's* article, "Picturesque Aspects of Farm Life in New York."[21]

III *Marriage*

Though Mary found it possible to pursue her art career while remaining on the family farm, she frequently sought the stimulation and encouragement of her city friends by inviting them to Milton for weekend visits. At times her company numbered those whose fame was already established: George Washington Cable came to the Hallock farm, as did George MacDonald and his wife. More often the visitors were younger figures: Helena and Richard, Elihu Vedder, Kate Bloede, Erhman S. Nadal. In her autobiography Mary gives these gifted companions their due, noting that they included "some of the most brilliant and fascinating young people of their time":

They might have stood for the artistic awakening in America. . . . In those early days the young poets were still on trial, the essayists and artists (except Vedder) in the stage called promising. . . . Reading of them later in far places where my life bestowed itself after marriage, I saw them—famous and bald and some of them fat—always as they were then; they had an immortality of youth for me.[22]

Occasionally Mary reciprocated by visiting in New York; and it was during one such stay, over the New Year's holidays of 1872-73, that she met Arthur De Wint Foote, her future husband. First cousin of Henry Ward Beecher and son of a member of the Connecticut legislature, Arthur came from a distinguished New England family. In 1866 he had entered Yale's Sheffield Scientific School for training in civil engineering but had later withdrawn on the unfortunate and erroneous advice of an ophthalmologist. When he met Mary, he was already convinced that he could succeed in his chosen profession without a degree; he was also certain that he loved her. During a special visit to her home that September, he reached a private understanding with her and then departed for the Far West. In Nevada and California he turned to what was then the most complex of all the mechanical arts—mining engineering. This new profession was considered glamorous and exciting, yet it demanded great versatility on the part of the practitioner. As Clark Spence has noted, the engineer's task "included locating, developing, exposing, measuring, and removing ore from the ground; he was charged with reducing metal from the ore and often with marketing it. He devised intricate machinery, became an expert in mining litigation, and frequently engaged in corporate promotion and investment."[23] By late 1875 Arthur Foote had completed his professional apprenticeship and had saved enough money to realize his goal of marriage. He wrote Mary that he was returning for her, and he arrived in Milton in February 1876.

Mary's feelings for her suitor were deep and disconcerting. As she had confided to Helena after Arthur's 1873 visit to Milton, love had come "unsought" while her mind

was fixed upon other people and other interests—It took possession of me unawares—I would not believe in it, or realize that my world and my life were changing—I clung to the old and doubted the new. . . until at last came a sudden light and happiness—tremulous, unreal—it lasted only a day or two in the happening—but it has gone to the roots of my life.[24]

Though she had faith in Arthur, she had misgivings about sharing his commitment to the West. She was, as she described herself, "born with roots which are always trying to grasp something and hold fast"; her intense attachment to the East, with its secure family ties and superior advantages for an aspiring artist, gave her pause.

One proof of her irresolution is "The Picture in the Fire-place Bedroom," the story she wrote to accompany an illustration for the February 1875 issue of *St. Nicholas Magazine.*[25] The tale is concerned with the narrator's recollection of a particular evening when, as a young girl, she had examined a painting in her grandmother's bedroom. While musing over the depiction of two children reading, she had fancied that the figures came to life, announcing their names as Dorothy and Walter Bourhope. Dorothy invites the narrator for a walk, and the two go "down a long hall, with many dim old pictures hung high above the wainscoting, and a row of deep windows, like the one we had just left, throwing broad bars of light across the floor" (250). When Dorothy disappears behind a tapestry to find a wrap for her friend, the narrator remains in the hall, futilely awaiting Dorothy's return. Although she awakens from her dream to discover the old picture unchanged, she is overwhelmed by a sense of lost opportunity (lost Bour*hope*). "I felt very still and cold, and somehow disappointed. If I had only raised that curtain a little sooner!"

The tale is fashioned from autobiographical elements, for Mary's grandmother had been a figure of romance to the young artist and her room, described in the *Reminiscences,* had often served as an inviting childhood retreat. Thus through its oneiric element Mary's first published piece conveys her attachment to the past and her anxiety about the future. By clinging to the security of her grandmother's world—the world of old portraits—Mary Hallock might be able to preserve the illusion of a timeless present. But by raising the curtain and crossing the threshold—by marrying a man committed to the West—she would not be able to control or predict the outcome. Though the ending of the story stresses the narrator's regret at not venturing into the unknown, it emphasizes equally the beautiful, leisurely past with which she feels secure.

On a wet, windy day some twelve months after her story appeared, Mary raised the curtain on a new life. She married Arthur Foote on February 9, 1876, in a quiet Quaker ceremony she later described:

. . .[T]he bride comes down the stairs unveiled and takes the arm of
the man who is waiting for her and they walk up the rooms unattended
to their places confronting the assembly, in a silence presumably given
to prayer (I remember hearing the rain drip from the trees outside):
then, taking each other by the hand, "In the presence of God, with
these our friends as witnesses," they pronounce the awful words which
in their case are considered irrevocable. It is not a moment one is likely
to forget.[26]

After a two-week wedding journey followed by her husband's
return to California, Mary faced the difficult task of preparing
for transcontinental transplantation. Questioning the "dark
stream of fate" ahead, she revealed to Helena the depth of her
concern: "That silly trembling feeling *inside* that I used to have
for days before I was married has come back again, and takes my
strength. I feel as if I were going to jump in the river trusting to
the chance of my knowing how to swim." Her qualms persisted
through the long days prior to her July departure: "No girl ever
wanted less to 'go West' with any man, or paid a man a greater
compliment by doing so."[27]

Once she began the overland journey, however, it was with
spirit and resolve—and with the aid of a servant whom she
proposed to use as a model in the many illustrations already
commissioned for that year. For it was in the dual role of artist
and wife that Mary Hallock Foote approached the West. The
frontier awaited, and would soon awaken to the power of her
pen.

CHAPTER 2

Apprenticeship

I   New Almaden and Santa Cruz

Frontier is a beautiful word, full of history and romance. To the young
men of all the generations it has been a challenge and a lure. The East
was East, in my time, and the West was the Far West; and the frontier
meant placer gold and lumber and wheat and of course land—all you
could grasp and hold. It meant "go West, young man." The young man
went and the woman followed—around the horn, across the Isthmus, by
the covered wagon trail.[1]

THUS wrote Mary Hallock Foote when she was nearing eighty
years old, romancing the long journey thousands of easterners had taken during the latter half of the nineteenth century.
As the twenty-eight-year-old bride of a California engineer, she
had followed her young man, crossing the continent in seven days
via train and stagecoach. "Home," once she joined Arthur in July
1876, was the small mining community of New Almaden,
California, located some fifty miles southeast of San Francisco.
The town of 1,000 was, as Mary quickly perceived, rigidly
stratified according to social class: the professional geologists
and engineers, along with the administrators of the mines,
formed the upper echelon. To this group Arthur belonged by
virtue of his position as resident engineer of the large New
Almaden Quicksilver Mine. The next stratum was formed by the
Cornish miners, followed by the Mexican miners and then by the
Chinese laborers.

While the Footes chose to cultivate few friends in New
Almaden, the community's proximity to San Francisco made it
possible for them to form a close, lasting relationship with their
relatives in the city, James and Mary Foote Hague. Hague, who
had secured for Arthur the New Almaden position, was one of

the most influential mining consultants in the West, and he aided his brother-in-law's career by introducing him to his own distinguished friends and colleagues. Likewise, Mary Hague ministered discreetly yet sympathetically to Mary Hallock Foote's initial needs, attempting to ease the shock of transplantation. As Mrs. Hague shrewdly observed apropos her sister-in-law, "Plant a wild-flower that has grown up under the shelter of New England rocks and woods out in the midst of a glaring, level valley in California, and it will either change its nature or die— either way the poor flower is very much bewildered."[2]

Mary Hallock Foote's introduction to western living was a large, one-room redwood-lined cabin atop a hill in the Santa Clara valley, with her only companion the servant girl who doubled as a model for her drawings. Arthur rarely was home, even for dinner, because he worked long, grueling hours at the mine. "What he called interesting," Mary later recalled,[3] "was to breakfast by candlelight at 3:00 A.M. and go underground and remain there, stooping at a transit in low dark drifts, till after midnight of the following night, a twenty-hour shift, and crawl home nearly blind with eyestrain, and call it a day." Left largely to her own resources, Mary Hallock Foote tried to stave off homesickness by making preparations for the arrival of her first child, due in April, and by dedicating herself to her art.

Her resultant drawings for Longfellow's *The Skeleton in Armor*, a ballad of Norse life, solidly established her credentials as an artist of male figures and evidenced unmistakable growth. Her greatest artistic achievement of this period, however, was her series of illustrations for a giftbook edition of *The Scarlet Letter*. The girl who early had been filled with awe by the writings of Hawthorne was, within the space of a few years, enhancing his talent with her own and winning him new readers. Howells, in an enthusiastic review of the Hawthorne edition, praised Foote as "the artist who perhaps unites more fine qualities than any other," and claimed that one particular illustration was "as yet quite unapproached in power by anything in American illustrative art."[4]

When not occupied with her commissioned drawings, Foote frequently entertained herself and her eastern friends with informal sketches and descriptions of the "strange, dear, horrid little place" she temporarily called home. Helena and Richard, receiving many of her lively letters, responded with an enthusiasm born not only of close friendship but also of discerning literary judgment. After suggesting that Mary prepare for *Scribner's* some illustrations of New Almaden with an accompanying article, they were not daunted by her modest demur. They fashioned from her letters an essay which Mary revised,[5] and Gilder published it in 1878, heralding the beginning of Foote's career as an author-illustrator of the West.

"A California Mining Camp" is a first-person account of those aspects of New Almaden which Mary Hallock Foote assumed would be picturesque to her eastern readers. It is not the Cornish camp or even the Chinese settlement which receives attention, but rather the Mexican population. Attracted and repulsed by their languid manner, the author offers interesting, brief sketches of the life led by the Mexican miners, woodpackers, bread deliverers, junk dealers—and by their women and children. These figures seem to blend into the natural setting provided by the New Almaden landscape and to accept unquestioningly the relentless dry season which baffles the narrator.

Foote's ambivalence toward her material is evident in the tone of the article:

Toward the close of the dry season, when brown and dusty August burns into browner, dustier September, a keen remembrance of all cool, watery joys takes possession of one's thoughts. The lapping of ripples in pebbly coves, the steady thump of oars in row-locks, the smell of apple blossoms on damp spring evenings, old millraces mossy and dripping, the bleating of frightened lambs at a sheep-washing and the hoarse, stifled complaint of their mothers mingled with the rushing of the stream,—all these once common sounds and sights haunt the memory. Every day the dust-cloud grows thicker in the valley, the mountains fade almost out of sight against a sky which is all glare without color; a dry wind searches over the bare, brown hills for any lingering drop of moisture the sun may have left there; but morning and evening still keep a spell which makes one forget the burden of the day.[6]

The nostalgic remembrance of apple blossoms and of bleating lambs contrasts with the ominous description of the western landscape. The mountains convey "the same feeling, whether dark with cloud-shadows or gorgeous in sunlight, the sense of a silent irresistible fate—waiting there, patient, unpitying, eternal." Drawn as it is from private letters written during her first prolonged absence from Milton, the essay reflects what Helena Gilder later termed "the difficulty of the daughter of the soil, whose people for generations had lived in and loved the river country of the East, to adapt herself to her new surroundings."[7] It represents, in short, Foote's first literary confrontation with the West.

The New Almaden experience lasted little more than a year for Mary; in September 1877 Arthur resigned his position in favor of accepting free-lance engineering assignments out of San Francisco. The Footes determined that Mary, with their four-month-old son, Arthur Burling Foote, should move to a boarding house in Santa Cruz, a coastal town southwest of New Almaden where families could live inexpensively. Arthur, when time and money permitted, joined them on weekends.

For Mary, the Santa Cruz stay proved emotionally draining: "I did a good deal of. . .[waiting] that winter, sitting on the bench and watching the 'vacant smiling seas.'" Her letters to Helena during this time recount frankly her discontentment with the West. At one point she confided,

We have planned our future in the crazy ways people do "when hope looks true and all the pulses glow." Ten years on this coast and then *home*. Is ten years an eternity?. . . [W]ill we be Western and "brag" about this glorious country—and the general superiority of half civilized over civilized societies? That sounds bitter. There are such good people here but I *can't* care for them. I am too old to be transplanted. The part of me which friendship and society claim must wait or perish in the waiting. The part of me which my work claims will plod on in a dogged way. If I do anything worthwhile it will be because of the encouragement I get. There is very little joy in it. . . .[8]

During this period it proved fortunate that Mary's work "plodded" so successfully—the *Scarlet Letter* illustrations alone netted $600—because the months following the move from New Almaden were not lucrative for Arthur. Though the money Mary earned was by mutual consent hers and was usually earmarked for savings, it went at that time to pay the bills in Santa Cruz. Fiercely loyal to her husband during this difficult period, Mary wrote defensive letters to Helena and Richard, reassuring them of Arthur's probity:

I know you cannot help worrying a little about us—but you musn't.
Arthur will not use my money and he is perfectly able to take care of
me. I did feel a little scared because I come of such cautious slow-
moving blood. He is different, but though he dares more than I, he is as
firm and steady as a rock and my faith not only in his utter honesty and
parity, but his power, grows every day.[9]

She admitted, however, that her drawings were "a great
help . . . in an emergency like this."
    The only nonfiction which Foote began during the Santa Cruz
period was an illustrated article for *Scribner's* entitled "A Sea-
port on the Pacific." The essay is one for which Foote took many
notes, for she incorporates into her account interesting historical
data about the area's early settlers. The editorial "we" is invoked
for narrative purposes, the passages of landscape description are
studded with botanical information, and the western scene is
frequently compared with that of the East. In the final analysis,
however, the essay fails; it neither sustains the reader's interest
nor rings with authorial conviction. Its most spirited element is
the conclusion:

It is true that society in the West does not hide its wounds so closely as
in the East, but is there not hope in the very fact of this openness? At
all events the worst is known. The East constantly hears of the
recklessness, the bad manners, and the immorality of the
West, . . . but who can tell the tale of those quiet lives which are the
life-blood of the country,—its present strength and its hope in the
future?
    The tourist sees the sensational side of California—its scenery and
society; but it is not all included in the Yo Semite guidebooks and the
literature of Bret Harte.[10]

While this final passage is stirring, it is unconvincing in context,
for it introduces an unmotivated tonal shift from objective
exposition to defensive apology. It suggests that Foote, herself
overly sensitive to the deficiencies of the West, strove to
compensate by undertaking a last minute defense of the very
cause she doubted.
    An equally guileless yet more personal composition dating
from the Santa Cruz period is "How Mandy Went Rowing with
the 'Cap'n,'" published in *St. Nicholas Magazine*. The first in a

series of children's tales which Foote would write over the next twenty years and into which she would incorporate family experiences and personalities, its setting is not coastal California but rather the familiar Hudson River country of her childhood. The brief story relates the experience of Mandy Lewis, who resents baby-sitting her infant brother and envies the freedom of her older brother. One afternoon, tiring of her responsibility, she leaves the baby protected near the water's edge and invites herself along on a rowboat trip with her brother and his friends. When the ride takes longer than expected, her pleasure in the excursion turns increasingly to concern. Fleeing the boat at her first opportunity, she returns to the dock to find her wildest fears confirmed: the baby is nowhere to be seen. The story ends with Mandy's joyful discovery that the infant is safe nearby and with her sincere change of heart: "Many times after that, the baby was a 'bother' to Mandy, but she was never heard to call him so."[11]

Behind this juvenile tale, with its homiletic conclusion, is Mary Hallock Foote's constructive working into fiction of her real-life dissatisfaction. Tucked away in Santa Cruz, Mary, like Mandy, was forced by her sex and age to assume the role of onlooker rather than participant; living apart from her husband of less than two years and burdened by new maternal responsibilities, she was unprepared for the occasional tedium of parenthood. In a letter to Helena she reported an acquaintance's remark that "I never seemed really to enjoy little Arthur" except when Arthur visited on weekends: "And it was perfectly [true]. The child was a plaything—a joy and a joy only when Arthur was along to make me feel young and gay. It is not a reasonable feeling but you know it as well as I."[12] Thus, in this early composition Foote transmuted into fiction the tensions created by her new circumstances. As the conclusion of "How Mandy Went Rowing with the 'Cap'n' " indicates, however, the author questioned but did not shirk the feminine role dictated by genteel tradition.

Foote's most significant—and personally revealing—piece of writing from the Santa Cruz period is a tale begun in 1877 to which she added a second part in 1878. She submitted the fiction, her first "mature" short story, not to Gilder but to William Dean Howells, editor of the *Atlantic:*

When Mr. Howells took my first story, he had complained in his charming way that it was "too wantonly sad" (one never forgets the words of a first "acceptance"). Keen to win his entire approval, I set to work and added a second part ending in happiness and the rains! As at first written it was a dry-season episode, breaking off on a minor key as such an episode would in a place like New Almaden. He took the second part, rather gloomily—he said it was "good, but not as good as the first part."[13]

Although not published until 1881, "In Exile" occupies a pivotal position in Foote's early writing and serves as the archetype for several of her subsequent tales.

The story chronicles the relationship over a period of eighteen months between Frances Newell, a schoolteacher, and Arnold, a mining engineer. Drawn together by homesickness in a small California mining town, the two measure the disparities between the cultivated civilization they left behind on the Atlantic coast and the crude one before them. Arnold, who has been in the West two years, endures the discomforts of mining life in anticipation of the day when he can afford to bring back his eastern sweetheart. Inwardly, however, he questions the propriety of uprooting his fiancée from all her associations, considering it male selfishness to do so. Anxious to receive Frances's opinion as to the effect of western transplantation on sensitive women, he discusses the question with her in general terms, without revealing that he is engaged. He suggests to the school teacher that for an eastern woman to come West means "the absolute giving up of everything. You know most women require a background of family and friends and congenial surroundings; the question is whether *any* woman can do without them."[14]

Frances's response—that the West "is the kind of place a happy woman might be very happy in; but if she were sad—or disappointed—she would die of it!"—reflects her own case. As the year passes and Arnold's attentions become less frequent, Frances pines away. Having found no reason to stay, and having learned from another of Arnold's commitment to the eastern girl, she makes plans to leave. When she tells him of her decision to accompany an invalid friend to the East, he informs her of his impending marriage. During the ensuing weeks, however, a series of forced incidents ultimately brings them together: Arnold's proposal is rejected, his sweetheart refusing the sacrifice implied, while Frances falls victim to a long fever and her invalid friend dies. When the two exiles next meet, both are conscious of a new loneliness: "We are cut off from everything," Frances says, while "an alternative had presented itself to [Arnold] with a pensive attractiveness,—an alternative unmistakably associated with the fact that the schoolmistress was to remain in her present isolated circumstances" (47–48). Several months later, during the first rain after the dry season, he proposes and she accepts.

"In Exile" introduces two important themes which are continued with slight variation through several subsequent Foote stories: feminine sacrifice and marriage by default. The former is only adumbrated, as in the conversations between Arnold and Frances. The fear expressed by Arnold that western life may demand considerable sacrifices on the part of an eastern woman becomes an established certitude in successive works; by 1889 the concern has been transformed into an authorial conviction: "When an Eastern woman goes West, she parts at one wrench with family, clan, traditions, clique, cult, and all that has hitherto enabled her to merge her outlines—the support, the explanation, the excuse, should she need one, for her personality."[15]

More fully developed in this early work is the pattern of the "default" theme, which depicts the romantic relationship between two young, attractive, and educated individuals. Born in the East but living in the West, the hero and heroine seem ideally suited because of shared interests and sympathies, yet there is always a complication which prevents them from achieving a satisfying relationship—a previous commitment, an obstacle presented by profession or family. It is only when the circumstances are suddenly altered through natural disaster, illness, death, or repudiation that they recognize the saving alternative each represents. Their resultant union is one of marriage by default.

It is this "default" element which especially distinguishes Foote's early stories from the welter of late nineteenth-century sentimental fiction and which leads to intriguing questions of a psychobiographical nature. Foote's writing in general, and "In Exile" in particular, is drawn largely from her personal experience; the character of Arnold, for example, is modeled after Arthur: such details as his eyestrain and smoking, his reserve and aloofness, and his one-room cabin built *away* from the camp confirm the resemblance. Similarly, Frances, like Mary, finds her boarding arrangement with a family rather uncomfortable, suffers from the strain of the dry season, and longs for her eastern home. Why then should Frances *reverse* her decision to return to the East? Why should she consider marrying someone who is irrevocably committed to the West? Foote provides her heroine with but one explanation: "I cannot go," she said. . . . "My friend does not need me now; she has gone home,—alone. She is dead!" (47). The loss of her only support, coupled with a debilitating illness, leaves her vulnerable, while her dependency arouses Arnold who, in losing his eastern sweetheart, has also suffered. Their betrothal is predicated on words of loss and compensation, not of love.

Through this pattern Mary Hallock Foote seems to be working out the change of circumstances and feelings which motivated her to marry Arthur. The "dark stream of fate" which brought them together was fed by mutual vulnerability as well as attraction. Her age, and the engagement of Richard and Helena, may have suggested to her that replacements for old friends and loyal suitors would be increasingly difficult to find. Likewise Arthur, laboring under a professional handicap (the lack of a formal college degree) which committed him to the West rather than the East, must have known there would be a scarcity of eligible matches on the frontier. Romantic love is never an analytical or rational process, but the business of Victorian marriage often was. "I wrote him, in defiance of fate, everything I was doing and all that happened to show that my life in the East was not made up of waiting, that it was going forward by leaps and bounds in a direction which did not point to marriage," recalls Mary in her *Reminiscences* (101). "I *must* go home. . . . I am to spend a month in Santa Barbara, and escort an invalid friend home. I shall have to say good-by, now," explains Frances to Arnold (36; 38–39). Yet in both cases circumstances change the status quo—and an alternative presents itself with "pensive attractiveness."

While the subdued passion of the lovers in "In Exile" and their marriage by default is a theme which Foote may have drawn from her experience unconsciously, she drew upon her emotional associations for the seasonal imagery deliberately. Frances's listlessness during the first dry season and her feverish state during the second parallel Foote's own dispirited response to the

California climate. For both women, the dry season is a metaphor
not only for individual discomposure but also for emotional
drought:

It was her [Frances's] second summer in California, and the phenomenon of the dry season was not so impressive on its repetition.
She had been surprised to observe how very brief had been the charm
of strangeness, in her experience of life in a new country. She began to
wonder if a girl, born and brought up among the hills of Connecticut,
could have the seeds of *ennui* subtly distributed through her frame, to
reach a sudden development in the heat of a California summer. She
longed for the rains to begin, that in their violence and the sound of the
wind she might gain a sense of life in action by which to eke out her dull
and expressionless days. (22)

That the tale closes with a violent downpour which precipi-
tates—and underscores—the lovers' avowal speaks more of
Foote's predilection for water imagery than of her acquiescence
to literary convention. The aridity of the West baffled and
repelled her; she was accustomed from childhood to the ponds
and freshets of the Hudson River countryside, to its summer rains
and winter storms. Water had always evoked a strong response
from her; its beauty and intensity fascinated her, as Wallace
Stegner observed in *Angle of Repose,* whether it took the form of
"rain in the face" or "exciting crossings of the Hudson through
floating ice."[16] In writing "In Exile" and other early stories with
landlocked western settings, Foote often relied on rainstorms to
convey energy and emotional release. In her later works and in
her correspondence, rivers and seas would figure prominently,
with water frequently symbolizing mystery, treachery, and final
escape.

When, in 1878, prudence counseled a return to Milton, Mary
was ready to embrace the opportunity. Arthur had accepted an
engineering assignment in Deadwood, South Dakota, where
neither safety nor comfort could be assured; he was to send for
the family as soon as conditions permitted. In the meantime, it
was desirable as well as economical that Mary and the baby go
"home." There both would be welcome, and there the fledgling
author would find sufficient emotional security to reexamine,

through writing, the significance of her first sustained contact
with the West.

II *Milton*

Mary Hallock Foote, in returning to Milton in March of 1878,
anticipated that she might be summoned to join her husband by
the end of the summer, but their reunion was postponed once
Arthur discovered that South Dakota offered no long-term
professional opportunities. Colorado held better potential for
engineer and prospector alike; so Arthur moved to Denver and
"work flowed in," but the Footes' future remained unsettled. Out
of this unexpectedly prolonged separation came some of the best
tales and illustrations of Mary's "early" period. Her surge of
creativity is perhaps best explained by the conducive conditions
she found at home. Freed from the anxieties and aggravations of
a foreign locale, and surrounded by protective relatives, Mary
Hallock Foote found the tranquillity so vital to her best art.

While she produced both a children's story and a descriptive
essay about New Almaden during her year-long Milton stay, her
better work in art as well as literature returned to the East for its
theme. Her illustrations for J. G. Holland's "The Puritan Guest"
and for John Burroughs's "Pastoral Bees" are accomplished and
convincing, while her drawings for Burroughs's "Our River,"
begun at this time, rank among her top illustrating achievements.[17] Her short story of note, "Friend Barton's 'Concern,'"
also reflects a return to material she could treat with familiarity
and confidence.

The tale draws upon the activities and traditions central to
Mary's Quaker heritage and uses numerous details of Hallock
family life. The "concern" of Mary's Uncle Nicholas, who had
preached at the Annual Meeting against the evils of slavery; the
frail health of her mother; her father's unsuccessful management
of the family property; the Hallock role during wartime—all are
skillfully incorporated. Yet "Friend Barton's 'Concern'" is
neither a family chronicle nor a Quaker tale, per se. When
relatives took Mary to task for the "unwonted and rather
shocking exposure, the exploitation in print of the faith of our

common ancestors,"[18] they missed the real point of the story. The piece deals only nominally with Barton's religious concerns; rather, the courtship of his daughter serves as the focus. While overtly the story relates Dorothy's changing attitude toward Walter Evesham—from aloofness through resistance to eventual acceptance—beneath the surface Foote is again using fictional characters named "Dorothy" and "Walter" ("Fire-place Bedroom") to explore certain aspects of the courtship of Mary and Arthur. Like "In Exile," it is another recounting of marriage by default.

The events of the tale unfold between the spring and fall of 1812 in a rural setting patterned after the Hudson River countryside. Thomas Barton, convinced that America should not war with England, determines that he must air his "concern" at the yearly meeting of the Society of Friends. Entrusting his mill and farm to the care of nineteen-year-old Dorothy, he departs for Baltimore. Although Dorothy receives little assistance from her infirm mother or her carefree younger brothers, she is too proud to accept aid from Evesham, a young miller who is renting the Barton ponds. When Evesham's business increases and the financial prospects of the Barton family rapidly diminish, Dorothy redoubles her efforts to spurn the miller's attentions.

A relationship between the two does not develop until fate interposes in the guise of a dangerous September rainstorm. Evesham rescues Dorothy and her family from their unsafe farmhouse and shares with them the comfort of his own home. The move proves a boon to courtship, for the Bartons' stay is extended several weeks because of the uncertain health of Dorothy's mother. With ample time to ponder her future, Dorothy at last acquiesces to Evesham's proposal of marriage; however, she shyly but stubbornly refuses to admit her affection for him. "Do you hate me now, Dorothy?" "Not so much as I did then."[19] Dorothy's suddenly reduced situation—she can depend upon neither her father nor her mother—flatters Evesham's masculine self-sufficiency while it limits her range of action and leads to marriage by default. The story concludes with Thomas Barton's return to his wife and daughter, still lodged in the Evesham home, and his response to Mrs. Barton's plea that Dorothy be permitted to marry "out of meeting":

Friend Barton raised his head: "Rachel," he said, "look at that!" He pointed upward to an ancient sword with belt and trappings which gleamed on the paneled chimney-piece, crossed by an old queen's-arm. Evesham had given up his large, sunny room to Dorothy's mother, but he had not removed all his lares and penates.

"Yes, dear; that's his grandfather's sword—Colonel Evesham, who was killed at Saratoga."

"Why does he hang up that thing of abomination for a light and a guide to his footsteps, if his way be not far from ours?"

"Why, father! Colonel Evesham was a good man. I dare say he fought for the same reason that thee preaches, because he felt it to be his duty." (123–24)

Barton's objections are silenced, with the reader learning in the final paragraph that fifty years later Dorothy Evesham will lose a grandson at Shiloh.

While this brief tale, like "In Exile," features subdued, passionless lovers, in spirit it is a *defense* of their marriage. That Dorothy's reticence before the grandson of Colonel Evesham mirrors Mary's reluctance before the son of Colonel Augustus Foote is confirmed by a passage from Foote's autobiography:

He unpacked his leathery luggage in the room we still called "grandmother's room" and laid his pipe and pistol on the bureau where her chaste neckerchiefs had been wont to lie, and he was as much of an anomaly in that house as if he had been a Viking himself or a man in armor. He came armed, in fact, with decision where indecision awaited him, and of course he carried the day.[20]

Back with her parents for an indeterminate period after twenty months of conjugal life, Mary responds in this tale to certain real or imagined criticisms of her marriage. From the limited perspective of the Milton Hallocks, Arthur's very worldliness—his seemingly incessant quest for a better position and the momentous traveling such a search entailed—was, if not suspect, incomprehensible. The newly married author couched her response in the terms most readily understandable to her skeptics—as a difference of religious opinion between two generations. In the fictional version Dorothy wins the argument, with her parents at last acknowledging Evesham's worth. The concluding sentence, however, suggests authorial reservation: "She has found the cool grays and the still waters; but on Dorothy's children rests the 'Shadow of the Sword'" (126).

What effect *would* the world symbolized by Arthur's pistol, the world of the frontier, have on their son and on the next generation? Young Arthur Burling Foote was very much on

Mary's mind as she finished "Friend Barton's 'Concern,'" for as
the old year gave way to the new the strain of separation wore
heavily upon her. In February, when Arthur proposed that she
leave the infant in Milton and join him in Leadville, Colorado,
the invitation was difficult to refuse. Convinced by her husband
that "Leadville at present was not a place for babies" and
bolstered by "[a]ll the wives and mothers at home . . . saying it
was 'the right thing to do,'" Mary Hallock Foote made the
decision—unusual for the period—to go.[21] Yet at the last moment
fate intervened: in March, on the very day she was to leave, her
son became seriously, then gravely, ill with white fever. It was a
full two months later before Mary, at last assured that Arthur
Burling's recovery was complete, could join her husband.

Mary assuaged her disappointment over the thwarted reunion
with Arthur by transmuting the episode into fiction. She must
have found writing a successful therapy, for she worked with
unusual rapidity and completed "A Story of the Dry Season"
before she arrived in Leadville. As in "In Exile," the central
metaphor is one of emotional enervation during the long western
dry spell, with the barren landscape underscoring the characters' need to form nurturing, sustaining relationships.

The principal figure of the tale is Gertrude Ellison, a young
matron boarding in the California town of San Miguel (Santa
Cruz) while her husband manages a mine in Nevada. Cut off from
family and friends in the East, she zealously devotes most of her
time during this waiting period to her baby daughter, Maude.
She economizes in small ways, refusing to hire a nurse for the
child and purchasing a secondhand crib. The latter savings
proves disastrous, for the original occupant of the crib died of a
contagious fever. Dr. Benedict, the local physician who attended
the young Mexican victim and saved his teenaged sister,
Mercedes, had ordered that the crib be burned; too late he
learns it has been sold to Mrs. Ellison. When Maude contracts the
fever, he feels a particular responsibility to save her.

The battle for the child's life is waged over three weeks in late
September and October; as mother and doctor spend long hours
together during the hot, dry season, Benedict falls in love with
the unsuspecting young matron. Robert Ellison arrives in
November, having come to his wife's side as quickly as he could,
and recognizes at once what Gertrude still fails to see. Thinking
that the baby's illness and the one-sided infatuation would never

have happened but for their "wretched, unnatural separation,"[22] Ellison urges his wife and child to return with him to Nevada. Gertrude consents, but after learning from Benedict that the baby's health will not withstand the journey, she finds herself torn by the conflicting claims of husband and child. Unaware that Benedict's prognosis is self-interested, she accepts his verdict; Ellison reluctantly departs alone, leaving Gertrude upset and uncertain of her decision:

> Her mind was benumbed with following the endless, circuitous logic of the morning's talk, while, at intervals, piercing the dull pain of her mood, came the thought of another long waiting begun. This was the third year of her married life. She had seen her husband just three days out of the year, and these had been by no means the whitest in the brief calendar of their wedded life. She was deeply stung by the forbearance of his manner at parting. He had looked at her, positively, with compassion, as at one not willfully, but hopelessly, astray. Her path had seemed very straight before her. Could anything be simpler than for a mother to guard her child's health? (779)

Her course becomes clear when Benedict, determined to salvage his self-respect, reverses his decision. Mrs. Ellison overtakes her husband in San Francisco, and the tale concludes lamely with Benedict deciding that he is in love with Mercedes.

"A Story of the Dry Season" is well paced and interesting, yet considered as literary art it does not rise above mediocrity. Foote's descriptions of the Santa Cruz beach, of the old mission, and of the priest's garden are authentic, and many of the minor incidents of the story have a germ of truth. But the tale is a weak repetition of the "In Exile" formula: Gertrude's homesickness suggests Frances Newell's longing for the East; Maude's illness recalls that of Frances; Ellison's total immersion in his profession echoes Arnold's; the obligatory storm breaking the dry spell occurs. Even the pattern of circumstances which conditions the hero or heroine to relinquish previous hopes is here, but with a difference. The alternative is implausible. Benedict, thwarted like Arnold in attaining the woman he desires, turns to a figure inferior to him in every respect—a "very strange little girl" who "looked, indeed, scarcely fifteen." The figure of Mercedes is hastily and briefly drawn; never significant at the beginning, her stature is even less credible at the end. Why then does Foote close the tale with their betrothal? Perhaps she resolved to

employ a "happy" ending since Howells had chided her for the
original low-keyed conclusion of "In Exile." Perhaps she wished
to complete the characterization of Benedict by exposing him as
a man of bad judgment as well as an individual capable of
treachery. Whatever her motivation, she must not have been
pleased with the results. Many years later, returning to the tale
to consider its inclusion in her first volume of short stories, she
chose to leave the piece uncollected; it had served an earlier
therapeutic purpose, and that was enough.

III *Leadville*

When Mary joined Arthur in Leadville in May 1879, she was
immediately captivated by the picturesque mining town nestled
in the Rocky Mountains at an altitude of 10,200 feet. In letters to
Helena she mused on the isolated grandeur of the town's natural
setting:

The snow peaks, with the shadow of the opposite range climbing their
sides at sunset, leaving their gleaming sierras in a sharp light against the
sky. The lonely trail winding wearily—lost, reappearing—disappearing
at last—enfolded in the long spurs of the range descending into the
valley, vanishing at the entrance to the pass. There is an awful temerity
in the advance of a handful of men with their flimsy accompaniments
into these solitudes. . . .[23]

The discovery of silver ore deposits having occurred two years
earlier, Leadville was rapidly being transformed from a sleepy
settlement into a bustling community by the time of Mary's
arrival. The official census in December 1878 was 5,040; by the
following November unofficial estimates placed the population
around 25,000–30,000. During the peak of the Leadville boom,
there were 100 new arrivals to the town each day.[24]
While Leadville attracted mining engineers and geologists,
attorneys and assayists, investors and promoters, speculators and
claimjumpers, as well as pioneering members of the fairer sex,
Mary was not often exposed to the raucous, exuberant life of the
town. Even though she is reported to have been the first woman
to descend into and explore a Colorado mine, she termed herself
"one of the 'protected' women of that time."[25] Insulated
according to the genteel conventions of the time, she pursued

most of her daily activities within the secure environs of a one-room log cabin, with visits from Arthur's associates and eastern friends providing frequent diversion.

The Leadville stay offered Foote a salutary change from the monotony of Milton and became for her a sort of holiday. Enjoying the renewed companionship of her husband and the respite from her maternal duties, she chose not to write, preferring merely to accumulate and bank her impressions of the strange new locale. She dedicated much of her time to executing art commissions previously received and to participating, with Arthur, in a social life built around a select circle of eastern friends. Her daily schedule, as she described it in a letter, was pleasantly frenetic:

We take our breakfast in the cabin and I am the maid of all work. It is a little place, but it takes some time to make it perfectly neat, as a little place must be, to be endurable. I *must* draw during most of the day. I have a good many calls and we dine downtown, not getting home till eight o'clock generally and almost always accompanied by one or more friends. I have no evenings, literally.[26]

Among the Footes' visitors were Clarence King and the distinguished men of his U.S. Geological Survey; U. S. Grant, Jr., whom they met through a neighbor; and Helen Hunt Jackson, who had recently published a children's novel about the Sangre de Cristo mining area of Colorado.[27] Idaho author Tom Donaldson also made a pilgrimage to the cabin, and his published memoirs indicate that Mary Hallock Foote's reputation as a hostess to cultivated society was not undeserved:

[Clarence] King and I forged along through a forest, crossed a mining ditch, and in a little clearing espied a cozy log cabin. As we approached, we discerned a rustic porch made comfortable by armchairs built of barrels sawed in half and stuffed with straw and covered by gunnysacks. To the right a hammock swung lazily, suggesting that an eastern woman, and a cultivated one, lived at the house.
. . . She was dressed in white and she rounded out a pleasing picture in contrast to rugged nature all about her home.
. . . Mrs. Foote settled herself for a chat until her husband returned, and my, my, how she did talk! She was well read on everything and ripped out an intellectual go-as-you-please backed up by good looks and brightness. She told us of their hopes, hers and Arthur's, in Mr.

Foote's engineering schemes. What was more interesting, she showed us some of her black-and-white illustrations for the work of other authors. She spoke of her early education at the Cooper Union Art School and of her childhood on the Hudson. . . . Love of nature was her dominant theme, and there was an evident contentment with her life, arduous as it must have been at times because of the lack of comforts and dearth of suitable female companions in Leadville.[28]

Donaldson's account of Foote as an engaging conversationalist accords with the descriptions of others who knew her. Her native shyness and manifest talent represented an intriguing combination; as James Herbert Morse later remarked, "for one whose name is so well known as writer and illustrator" Mary Hallock Foote retained her "ladylike, bashful ways and prettiness wonderfully well."[29]

As the summer of 1879 waned, the Footes' plans for the winter crystallized. Mary returned to their son in Milton, while Arthur closed their cabin for the winter and accepted a field position with the U.S. Geological Survey. The following spring he was offered the management of the Adelaide Consolidated Silver Mining Company, which comprised four mines in Leadville, so the Footes, with young Arthur Burling, returned in May 1880 to their housekeeping in "the little log cabin by the ditch." Mary's second stay in Colorado was unexpectedly short, however, for a confrontation between the miners and the mine owners proved fatal to the Footes' hopes of settling in Leadville. With Arthur joining other mine managers in rejecting union demands, there came a bitter three-week strike, followed by a hotly contested boundary dispute between the Adelaide and the Argentine, a rival mine. Mary wrote Helena of the excitement: "They have had actual war at the Adelaide. The Argentine had fifty men and forty stands of arms. The Adelaide has won the injunction suit and so I suppose quiet reigns . . . again. I am afraid of secret shots when Arthur or Van [Ferdinand Van Zandt, Arthur's subordinate] are riding by on their way to and from the mine."[30] The standoff between the two mines, lasting through the summer, so paralyzed the Adelaide's operations that at last the eastern owners ordered it shut down—giving Mary the material for *The Led-Horse Claim*, her first novel, but leaving Arthur without a position.

IV *Transition*

Mary Hallock Foote did not begin *The Led-Horse Claim* immediately, and it was ultimately a better work for her not having done so. Between September 1880, when she departed Leadville for Milton, and the winter of 1881–82, when she began her manuscript, she made two decisions which shaped the course of her writing career.

The second summer in Leadville had caused her to acknowledge the impossibility of continuing to meet illustration deadlines. She had, during the four months, nursed her son through a long bout of white fever, fallen ill herself, and suffered a miscarriage. Her husband's increasingly unsettled job situation and the family moves it necessitated further militated against her ability to execute art commissions on time. Moreover, she recognized the inherent difficulty of working with nonwestern material when she seemed fated to spend her time in the West: she had neither models nor costumes nor research materials upon which she could draw for inspiration. "Imagine illustrating *Lucile* for an edition de luxe in Leadville—I who had never been abroad in my life and didn't know even what sort of chairs they sat on at European watering places!"[31] For all of these reasons she determined that henceforth she would refuse time orders and illustrate chiefly her own works, on which no deadline would be imposed.

Foote's decision came at a time when her services as an illustrator were more highly sought after than ever before. Her contract for Bulwer-Lytton's *Lucile,* for which she had been forced to seek a deadline extension, had been a very prestigious commission. More meaningful to Foote personally, though, had been the order for Tennyson's *A Dream of Fair Women,* which had offered an opportunity to illustrate her favorite poet. But the Bulwer-Lytton and Tennyson texts, like almost all her orders during 1879–80, were period pieces demanding authentic detail. One need only compare Foote's western illustrations during this time—the series for Ernest Ingersoll's "The Camp of the Carbonates," for example—with one of her eastern productions—the drawings for the anonymous ballad *Aucassin and Nicollete*—to appreciate the differing nature of the demands each assignment placed upon the artist.[32]

The transition in Foote's art career from interpreting works written by other authors to concentrating on her own texts signaled a concomitant shift in her attention from drawing to writing. After 1880, with her time newly released from the demands of commission deadlines, she entered a period of increased productivity as an author. In the five years following the appearance of her "Fire-place Bedroom" story, she had composed only brief prose pieces; but between 1881–85 she published two full-length novels as well as a significant amount of shorter fiction. She later modestly claimed that this productivity grew from her "aborted art": "I found the West and its absorbing material too much for my pencil."[33]

Her increased interest in writing also stemmed from the fertilizing influence of a three-and-one-half-month sojourn in Mexico during early 1881. Through Helena Gilder's influence Arthur had been solicited to inspect some mines in Mexico, and Richard proposed that Mary prepare an illustrated travelogue of the journey. The scheme appealed very much to her romantic spirit. Raised in a family whose otherworldliness did not prize the opportunity of foreign travel, she nonetheless desired it intensely. To make the trip to Mexico struck both the Footes as frivolous, but it was a decision neither ever regretted. "I knew that we never had been anywhere before—we had merely romped about a bit in that 'historic vacuum' of the Far West," she wrote some fifty years later, revealing the tremendous significance which the experience still held for her:

. . . I am not sure but he [Arthur] took the job for its romance side for us both. We were no longer so very young, but we were still foolish. It came into our lives without a plan or prevision. . . . There it glows, a spot of intenser color in memory's painted windows that look toward sunset, riveting the eye amidst lower tones of burnt-out forests and dry deserts and old, fenced-in farms.[34]

From the Mexico experience Mary produced interesting travel accounts and some noteworthy illustrations; in fact, her first installment was chosen by Gilder as the lead piece in his debut issue of *Century Illustrated Monthly Magazine,*which succeeded *Scribner's* in November 1881. But the truly significant result of Mary Hallock Foote's trip was its stimulating influence upon her subsequent fiction. Enthralled by the ambience of Mexico, she returned in spirit to the romantic literature which had captivated her in her youth, rereading Tennyson and rediscovering Irving's Spanish legends. From these literary influences, and from the renewed confidence in herself and her marriage which the trip promoted, Mary Hallock Foote gathered newfound inspiration. She was ready to become a romancer.

When Mary and Arthur returned from Mexico, they altered their habits, as if to signify the infectious spirit of travel, by spending the summer not in New York but in Maine, on Deer Island in Penobscot Bay. During that vacation Foote began one of the best tales she ever wrote, "The Story of the Alcázar." Published in June 1882, it is a successful blend of New England setting with Old World (Spanish) romance and intrigue.

The narrative, which is related from an omniscient point of view, employs the framework of a tale within a tale: Captain John, a kindly resident of Deer Island, recounts to a boy on summer vacation the mysterious background of a foreign ship anchored in Penobscot harbor.[35] According to the veteran seaman, the vessel named the *Alcázar* (Moorish for "fortress-castle") had been abandoned long before 1827, when it drifted into the area and was towed into the harbor by one of the islanders, Captain Green. Green appropriated the vessel, a slaver with the skeletons of abandoned Africans still in the hold, and recommissioned it to run lumber between Bangor and New York. The events of the *Alcázar*'s maiden voyage confirmed the fears of its superstitious crew: three lives were lost, in addition to the deck cargo, and the ship was considered henceforth a "floating coffin." On its return, the *Alcázar* encountered a storm: Green, refusing to take cover, cried out to his crew, "I've got to go with her" and subsequently was swept overboard.[36] The remaining men survived, finding safety in the harbor.

The details of the phantom ship with its moribund crew and its captain guilty of blasphemy and doomed never to enter port are clearly inspired by the *Flying Dutchman* legend popularized during the nineteenth century by Wagner's opera. Although the *Alcázar* does not sail against the wind full-rigged as does its Germanic prototype, there lacks little else to complete the ominous parallel: Captain Green "was kind o' res'less and wakeful, walkin' the decks and lookin' over the stern at the big ship follerin' him like a ghost. The moonlight was a little dull with fog, but he could see her, plain, a-comin' on before the wind with her white riggin' and bare poles, and hear the water sousin' under her bows" (133). Rumored to have sailed slave-trading vessels in his youth, Green is thought by Captain John to have been the original master of the *Alcázar*. Short of water, the captain and his crew, the storyteller opines, must have abandoned the ship with its living cargo. As if to exact justice, the vessel went "a-huntin' him up and down the western ocean for twenty year, with them dead o' his'n in her hold" (144). Thus when the ship first appeared to Green outside the harbor, he knew he could not escape and resigned himself to a watery fate.

What lends this tale special interest and impresses the reader, ultimately, is not the grisly legend but rather Foote's delineation of Captain John and his New England setting. The "dark shapes of shadowy islands" thronging the harbor and the weather-beaten houses "crowded together on the brink of the cliff above the beach, looking like a group of hooded old women watching for a belated sail" (128) capture the expression of the islanders' lives. Chief among the "inmates" of the island is Captain John, whose moral sternness is tempered, in the end, by a suggestion of frailty. The reader discovers that Captain John, who at one point comments on the virtues of Mrs. Mary Spofford Green, has long nursed a secret affection for the woman who lived and died a slaver's wife:

On the gray beach below, a small, dingy yawl, with one sail loosely bundled over the thwarts, leaned toward the door-latch as if listening for its click. It had an almost human expression of patient though wistful waiting. It was the poorest boat in the Harbor; it had no name painted on its stern, but Captain John, in the solitude of his watery wanderings among the islands and channels of the bay, always called her the Mary Spofford. (145-46)

Like Green, Captain John in his final days admits only to himself his special vulnerability. Haunted yet consoled by his love for the wife of another, he is a memorable figure who remains with the reader and whose character is reinforced by the ground-swell imagery of the tale's conclusion:

[Captain John] parted with his young listener at the top and took a lonely path across the shore-pasture to a little cabin, where no light shone, built like the nest of a sea-bird on the edge of high-water mark. . . . There were voices, calling and singing abroad on the night air, reflected from the motionless, glimmering sheet of dark water below as from a sounding-board. Cow bells tinkled away among the winding paths along the low, dim shores. The night-call of the heron from the muddy flats struck sharply across the stillness, *and from the outer bay came the murmur of the old ground-swell, which never rests, even in the calmest weather.* (145-46; italics mine)

V   The Led-Horse Claim

With its Irvingesque approach to legend and its overtones of romance, "The Story of the Alcázar" was a fitting prelude to *The Led-Horse Claim: A Romance of the Mining Camps* (1883), the full-length Colorado fiction Mary Hallock Foote began after the summer in Maine, once Arthur had again departed for the West and she had returned to Milton with Arthur Burling. In subtitling her work a "romance," Foote not only was acknowledging her debt to the romantic literature which had enthralled her in her youth but also was carefully distinguishing the nature of her writing.

As a prose form, the romance can be traced to the long episodic tales of love and adventure found in Greek and Icelandic literature as early as the first century A.D. With its abstract setting, its emphasis on action rather than character, and its heavy reliance on external forces for resolution, the romance is usually uncritical in spirit, appealing to one's wishes rather than one's knowledge. A love story and a quest were central to the medieval romances, with the hero and heroine characteristically involved in a cyclical pattern of union, separation, and reunion. By the sixteenth century "love at first sight" was an integral element, and during the eighteenth century geographical setting evolved into a factor affecting character. By the second decade of the nineteenth century the novel had established itself as an immensely successful vehicle for the romance.

In early nineteenth-century American romances, the hero's course follows a predictable pattern: cut off or withdrawn from friends and loved ones, he undergoes a series of experiences which generally culminate with his reentry into society. A happy ending is indispensable. In succeeding decades the romance tradition of the American novel changed subtly. Under Edgar Allan Poe, Nathaniel Hawthorne, and Herman Melville, the account of the quest became more mythic and allegorical, less fettered by fact; the love interest was deemphasized. During the last third of the century, sentiment enjoyed a revival, with saccharine romances vying with works of dispassionate realism for best-selling honors.

In *The Led-Horse Claim*, Foote employed the romance form loosely, borrowing certain of the traditional formulas and rejecting others. The "moonlight and golden hair" elements were occasioned in part by the story's *donnée* as she explained to James Hague, her brother-in-law, "In the sentimental passages, I hope you will remember that I am not representing what I consider *ideal* relations, but the relation to each other of two *young*, isolated and passionate people—the people who would naturally fit in a story of crude action and rash sentiment."[37] Coexisting with the romance elements was Foote's own concern for fidelity—for realism of situation and detail.

In all but one respect, her realistic treatment of star-crossed lovers delighted the *Century* staff. Gilder was known to champion realism "just so long as it was romantic." He averred at one point, "The more reality the better! But let it be reality all the way through, reality of the spirit as well as of the flesh, not a grovelling reality which ignores the 'romantic spirit.' "[38] In the first draft of *The Led-Horse Claim*, Mary Hallock Foote ended the story the way she believed "it would have ended; the young pair would, in the order of things as they were, never have seen each other again. But my publisher wouldn't hear of that! I had to make a happy ending." She acceded to Gilder's demand but retained the novel's convincing central situation and setting; the result proved to be a modest best seller.

Reminiscent of *Romeo and Juliet* and Tennyson's *Maud: A Monodrama* in its theme of love in the midst of an interfamilial feud, *The Led-Horse Claim* recounts the courtship of George Hilgard, manager of the Led-Horse mine, and Cecil Conrath, sister to the manager of the rival Shoshone mine. That Hilgard is an heroic but ill-starred youth is made evident at the outset: "Had [he] been born ten or fifteen years sooner, he might have won more honor. . . . He would have been the idol of his men, the life of his mess."[39] When he meets Cecil, recently arrived from the East, the two fall in love at first sight. As tensions mount between the mines, the budding affair is threatened because of the respective allegiances of the lovers. The Led-Horse, contending that the Shoshone has been mining a vein of its ore, has obtained a court injunction preventing the Shoshone from continuing to mine the vein; the Shoshone must reclaim the vein by force or shut down. Alarmed by the violent nature of the dispute, Cecil pleads with Hilgard to leave the camp in order to avoid open confrontation with her brother Harry. But on learning that men of the Shoshone plan to break into his mine, Hilgard perceives his duty to be the mine's defense; with West, his loyal assistant, he forcefully repels the intruders. When Cecil learns that her brother Harry has been fatally wounded in the fight, she repudiates her erstwhile lover and returns to the East in mourning; Hilgard subsequently resigns from the Led-Horse to search for her. The tale ends with their subdued reunion and marriage, marred by the unrelenting enmity the Conrath relatives bear Hilgard.

As in previous writing, Foote found the germ for the novel in her own experience, remarking to Hague that she could "not write a story without seeing the places."[40] The actual episode was Leadville's Adelaide-Argentine mining dispute: in the story, Arthur's subordinate, Steve Fleming, becomes West while Ferdinand "Van" Zandt serves, with Arthur, as the model for Hilgard. In order to satisfy the demands of magazine serialization, Foote strove to include peaks of excitement, suspense, and surprise at regular intervals. Thus a series of contrived lovers' encounters generates the action of the tale but at the same time strains credibility. Cecil unsuspectingly happens on Hilgard at a camp social event, in the fields, and even underground in a mine. Equally implausible are the coincidental meetings which transpire after each departs Leadville. Gilder's editorial mandate to conclude the tale happily leads to the lovers unsuspectingly lodging in the same hotel, Hilgard being stricken by a fever, and Cecil nursing him back to health. When Cecil subsequently flees, protesting that theirs is an impossible love, the New York village where she lives turns out to be the very community to which Hilgard goes to visit relatives. The conclusion of the tale, though dictated by commercial interests, bears Foote's unmistakable imprint. Although the lovers marry, theirs may be regarded a union by default. Cecil accepts her "fate" only reluctantly, marrying in a small home ceremony on a wet windy morning.

While the characterization of the major figures in *The Led-Horse Claim* is unimaginative, the work is redeemed by several

original motifs which Foote introduces here and recurs to in
subsequent novels. One is the nature of the sensitive relations
between East and West. She avoids the error her successor,
Hamlin Garland, would make of oversimplifying the issue into a
formula of financial East against rural West; rather, by offering
authentic details and avoiding overstatement, she focuses on the
everyday problems of the relationship. Particularly convincing is
her presentation of the difficulties of managing a mine when one
is dependent upon the decisions of absentee investors and
subject to the inevitable delays of transcontinental communication; the mine owners are "half the width of the continent away"
(30) and "engaged in larger schemes, which made the fate of the
Led-Horse of comparatively little consequence" (33). Equally
persuasive is Foote's rendering of the circumstances surrounding
Conrath's burial in the West rather than in the East. When the
men of the Shoshone do not receive an immediate reply to their
telegram notifying Conrath's eastern relatives of his death, they
hastily and angrily assume the responsibility themselves. The
resultant funeral scene, with its romantic echoes of *Maud* and its
grimly absurd details, effectively conveys the tensions underly-
ing the western experience.

Another of Foote's motifs is the cumulative effect of the strains
of mining life on those who have journeyed West. Shocked that
one of her friends paid with his sanity for staying in Leadville
"too long,"[41] Foote peoples her novel with several "warped or
stale humanities." Doctor Godfrey, Hilgard's longtime friend,
has fallen victim to a slow but inevitable deterioration: "A
pervading seediness had crept over his outward man. The moth
of long isolation from gentle communications had corrupted his
good manners, and the thief of discouragement had stolen his
pride" (73). Likewise, Conrath pursues a vengeful course
incompatible with the refined lessons of his youth and falls prey
to excessive drinking. The deleterious influence of the West is
also felt by the women of Leadville. For Mrs. Denny, a young six-
months' resident of the camp, the change is "like a premature
blight on a still full-veined flower. Her youthfully rounded cheek
had a slightly crumpled texture, and her eyes, of the blue of
childhood, were too widely, restlessly expanded" (45).

Indirectly related to this deterioration is another motif—the
awesome forces of Nature. In a letter to Helena written while
revising the last chapters, Foote described the mountains

surrounding Leadville and noted, "There is something appalling to me in the blank silence of those immeasurable unrecorded ages that lie there exposed—no *not* unrecorded, but *I* cannot read their dumb tablets of rock."[42] Within the novel she depicts a force akin to this silence but more unsettling. When, in the central episode, Cecil descends into the Led-Horse mine, the heroine faces not the "sphynxlike calm" of the exposed mountains but the "subanimate mutterings" of their subterranean counterparts. Below ground, the rock is disturbingly active and oppressive:

There were far-off, indistinct echoes of life, and subanimate mutterings, the slow respirations of the rocks, drinking air and oozing moisture through their sluggish pores, swelling and pushing against their straitening bonds of timber. Here were the buried Titans, stirring and sighing in their lethargic sleep. . . . Left to their work, the inevitable forces around her would crush together the sides of the dark galleries, and crumble the rough-hewn dome above her head. Cecil did not know the meaning or the power of this inarticulate underground life, but it affected her imagination all the more for her lack of comprehension. (113–14)

Here is not only Nature's indifference but also its malign potential. Reduced to elemental form, Foote's presentation of man confronting destructive forces and deprived of all the safeguards of the old order is a literary rendition of the Darwinian struggle for survival. The altitude "acts like the law of natural selection on those who aspire to breathe its thin air, sparing only the sound of heart and lung, and fanning the nerve-fires into breathless, wasteful energy" (11). The "sanguine youth" of Leadville are saved; many of the "dangerous elements of the camp—the mud, the weeds, and the driftwood which would have choked a more sluggish current—" are swept aside (12); the old and infirm perish quickly. Thus there is death in the midst of life for many who journey to that "senseless, rootless place."[43]

When *The Led-Horse Claim* began appearing in installments in 1882, it was immediately popular, but Mary Hallock Foote protested its success with genuine modesty. To Hague she wrote of her "appalling impudence" in "daring to write and let things be printed on such a slip-shod basis of inaccuracies"; to Helena she affirmed her inadequacy. Disconcerted by the sudden attention, she declared to her confidante that she was "in no danger of being overwhelmed" by her " 'success' as a writer": "[W]hat with the consciousness of my limitations in art and the fact that I have somehow slipped . . . into a position where I lay myself open to comparison and criticism—I am not very happy in my work. . . ."[44] The literary reviews of Foote's accomplishments were far more lenient. As when her illustrations were first published and "flocks of pleasant notices arrived,"[45] her debut as a novelist was equally well received. The *Atlantic, Book-Buyer, Spectator*—all welcomed her contribution to western literature and expressed an expectation of more.

During 1882 and 1883, the recently acclaimed novelist found not only professional matters but domestic concerns competing for her attention. In September 1882 she gave birth to Elizabeth Townsend ("Betty"), a long-awaited daughter; the following spring she became pregnant again. In June 1883 Arthur departed for Boise, Idaho, to become the Chief Engineer and Manager of the Idaho Mining and Irrigation Company. The newly founded enterprise, as Mary learned from her husband's letters, gave every promise of success but required a long foreground—one which would necessarily involve his uninterrupted presence in Idaho for years. To Mary, the prospect of another prolonged separation was untenable, yet a move to the Boise desert rekindled all her old fears of deracination:

This meant farewell music, art, gossip of the workshop, schools that we knew about, new friends just made who would forget us, old friends better loved than ever and harder to part from—all the old backgrounds receding hopelessly and forever. . . . *I felt adrift,* as it were, cast off on a raft with my babies, swept past these wild shores uninhabited for us. My husband steering us with a surveyor's rod or some such futile thing—and where were we going on this *flood of uncertainties?* I was in that frame of mind and body that if my dreamer had been Moses I should have tried to stay his hand *lest the water when it followed his stroke might become a torrent and overwhelm us.*[46] (italics mine)

Troubled by dreams "of lonely rivers that hear no sound save their own dashings,"[47] Mary Hallock Foote nevertheless mastered her doubts and prepared for a fall departure. But in October the events of four years before repeated themselves: the westbound train departed without Mary, leaving Arthur to receive the disappointing news. Weakened by a miscarriage (the second of three she would ultimately suffer), the thirty-six-year-old wife and mother had been wisely counseled by family to mend her health before undertaking the move. When Arthur returned to Milton in the spring of 1884, the Foote family traveled to Idaho to begin what Mary would later term "our longest and hardest campaign, and the last one we ever attempted on our own initiative."[48]

CHAPTER 3

Desperate Romance

THE enterprise that attracted the Footes to Idaho—the reclamation and irrigation of the desert land between the Boise and Snake rivers—was an extremely costly and risk-filled venture directed by Arthur, supported in part by eastern capital and in part by the financial resources of friends and relatives. The projected system was to irrigate 600,000 acres of the Boise vicinity through a series of storage reservoirs, dams, and canals. To finance the first stage of construction, the newly formed Idaho Mining and Irrigation Company needed to raise nearly $1,500,000, while the cost of preliminary work alone amounted to $4,000 a month.[1]

The communality of the endeavor is best symbolized by the intense commitment of Mary's sister and her husband: leaving the familiar world of Milton behind, Bessie and John Sherman moved to Boise, shared a home with the Footes, and invested their savings in the project. While John joined Arthur in the irrigation work, Bessie freed her sister from many domestic concerns and served as a buffer between Mary and the raw town of 2,500 whose increasing efforts at polite socialization so fatigued her. Most important, Bessie's capable presence afforded Mary the opportunity to write for hours without interruption.

I John Bodewin's Testimony

Foote's first literary project after arrival in Idaho was the revision of a novel begun fitfully the year before. Another story of Leadville, the book struck Mary as "a superfluous thing to be doing in these days when every other person one has ever heard of is writing the novel of the period,"[2] yet she did not refrain from employing the romance formula or contemporary setting which had so recently brought her success. As in *The Led-Horse*

Claim, a mining dispute provides the background for *John Bodewin's Testimony* (1886): the Eagle Bird mine, owned by Mr. Newbold and prospering from a recent "find," faces a challenge of its boundaries by Colonel Billy Harkins, owner of the adjacent Uinta mine. Caught between the two sides is the novel's titular hero, a civil engineer from Connecticut.

"One of the most truthful, sensitive, and scrupulous of men,"[3] John *Tristram* Bodewin is also one of the most enigmatically passive—a knight manqué—and it is his motives for *not* acting which provide much of the tension of the novel. Sought by both mines as an expert witness because he had surveyed the claims a year earlier, he is reluctant to testify, for he knows Harkins's case to be unjust yet is indebted to him for kindness shown to his sister years before. Bodewin attempts to discharge the obligation by remaining silent, but he is forced to reassess his position as he becomes increasingly attracted to Newbold's daughter, Josephine, who has come West on a visit. Determining at last that he cannot "cancel a private debt by neglecting a public duty" (140), he agrees to testify on behalf of the Eagle Bird.

To prevent Bodewin from appearing in court, Harkins pays two mountaineers to kidnap him before the trial and to secrete him in their cabin for several days. The mountain interlude serves to develop Bodewin's innocent entanglement with Babe Keesner, the beautiful unlettered daughter of his captor. On the condition that he deny ever having known her family, she masterminds his escape, but the imprudence of Bodewin's assent soon becomes clear. The townspeople's suspicions are aroused when he cannot describe his captors, his friend Hillbury deserts his cause, and even Josephine's steadfast loyalty is tested when Babe Keesner trails Bodewin to the Eagle Bird and loses her life in the mine.

That Bodewin eventually clears his name and claims Josephine is a function of her strength of character rather than his, for he attempts to evade all action. His refusal to testify against the Keesners results in Harkins's legal victory and in his own flight from the mining community: "The trial scene had branded him for life. The infamy of it was known to but a few people, but it would spread. Already he could hear the story of it repeated in every city where he had ever been known" (326). Bodewin's wounded self-esteem permits him the luxury of sending a single letter of explanation, without return address, to Josephine after she returns to her home in Kansas City. The latter's happiness in learning the facts that vindicate her lover's conduct leads her to show the letter to Hillbury, through whose efforts Bodewin is located, the friends reconciled, and the lovers married. The tale concludes with Bodewin and Josephine journeying to the West to make their home.

The novel's setting and certain of the characters are drawn largely from the Footes' experiences in Leadville in 1879. Their log cabin becomes the home of one of the characters; Leadville's Clarendon Hotel is renamed the Wiltsie House; and members of the U. S. Geological Survey serve as models for their thinly veiled fictional counterparts. The inspiration for the trial scene, the "hardest part" of the novel for Foote to write,[4] was Arthur's participation as an expert witness in a Denver lawsuit in 1878. Hired by mine owner "Uncle Billy" Stevens, Arthur prepared convincing testimony which won the case. For his two months of efforts, which assured Stevens control of a $4 million mine, Arthur received only $100, thus prompting Mary to transform Stevens into "Colonel Billy" Harkins, the villainous plaintiff.

In *John Bodewin's Testimony*, Foote seems more certain of characterization than in her first novel. While Bodewin and Josephine function as conventional romance protagonists, their presentation suggests that Foote had absorbed her Hawthorne. The opening scene, detailing Bodewin's emergence from the darkened mouth of the mine into the "bleak untempered light" and on into the forest, presents him as "one whom life had refined and sobered" (11). His "singularly unaggressive" demeanor contrasts with the vivacity of Josephine, whom he encounters in a sunlit clearing in the woods. Just as the setting recalls *The Scarlet Letter*, so the subsequent characterization reinforces the Hawthornian overtones. Like the Reverend Dimmesdale, Bodewin is bowed by secret guilt and remorse; he, too, hides a heavy spirit beneath a clouded visage. His guilt stems not from an adulterous love affair but from culpability for his sister's ill-fated marriage and death. Bodewin, like Dimmesdale, has an exaggerated sense of obligation to his oppressor; his indebtedness to Harkins weighs heavily upon him and robs him of resilience. In the words of Hillbury, Bodewin suffers from a "want of grit" (102) which could easily lead to a deadly despondency.[5]

Josephine, whose manner is reminiscent of Hawthorne's Hester, counsels her lover to ignore his "morbid conscience" (144). It is she who recognizes that, in refusing to bury the past, Bodewin has estranged himself from the present: "He had waited long, had kept the chambers of his heart empty . . ." (131). Josephine urges Bodewin to confront the challenge presented by their mutual antagonist, but her courage, like that of Hester, does not prepare her for the "taint of moral poltroonery" (178), in Bodewin. His reluctance to act bewilders her, as does his determination to remain silent; nevertheless, she retains her faith in him even when he flees after the trial. By exhorting Hillbury to seek out Bodewin, she becomes, like Hawthorne's heroine, the moving force behind her lover's reconciliation with his fellow men.

When *John Bodewin's Testimony* appeared in print, its success confirmed Foote's position as a novelist of the West. The eastern establishment reviewed it favorably, while miners treated the author "as a compatriot and an old campaigner." Foote reported to Helena, "[T]hey send me newspaper accounts of murders and conspiracies connected with mining and land-grabbing, and want me to do justice to these happy themes."[6] Her readers recognized *John Bodewin's Testimony* as a more sympathetic portrayal of western life than its predecessor. In both novels major differences exist between the western miners and the eastern investors, but whereas in *The Led-Horse Claim* the miners take matters into their own hands, alienating the East and causing disastrous results, in *John Bodewin's Testimony* prudence and conciliation are the keynotes. By making the rival proprietors western men, and by resolving the dispute in a courtroom rather than in the mine shafts, the author attempts to enhance the credibility of the mining industry. As one of the characters explains, "We are Western men; we want to encourage Eastern capitalists to seek investments in the West. One way to do it will be to show them that their investments *in* the West can and will be protected *by* the West" (291). This spirit of conciliation between East and West is also manifested in the novel's lyrical conclusion. As Bodewin and his bride descend from a train to begin their new life together in the West, they are bathed in the dry, soft winds which had stirred Foote on her own arrival in Idaho five years before:

Wind of the great Far West, soft, electric, and strong, blowing up through gates of the great mountain ranges, over miles of dry savannah, where its playmates are the roving bands of wild horses, and the dust of the trails which it weaves into spiral clouds and carries like banners before it! Wind of prophecy and of hope, of tireless energy and desire that life shall not satisfy. Who that has heard its call in the desert, or its whisper in the mountain valleys, can resist the longing to follow, to prove the hope, to test the prophecy! (344)

What Foote demonstrates with this second Leadville novel is her kinship with the tradition of frontier fiction established by James Fenimore Cooper and Bret Harte. During the 1800's Cooper's Leatherstocking tales had popularized a number of conventions which most western romancers subsequently observed. Foremost was the requirement that the nominal hero be an easterner, a man of upper-class background who is thrust into an alien frontier setting. The tension between expectation and reality and the clash between rival value systems were to provide the story's crucial impetus. *John Bodewin's Testimony* fits this pattern, with the hero pitted against mountaineers rather than Indians. Cooper's formula similarly called for a refined eastern heroine, with western women and female Indians qualifying for admiration only, as Henry Nash Smith has commented, "in proportion as they have escaped from the crudity and vulgarity of their surroundings, either by virtue of birth elsewhere, or through the possession of an implausible innate refinement."[7] This convention is demonstrated by Bodewin's prejudice against Josephine, whose charms are rendered suspect by her origins: "Bodewin had not sought to see her or be presented to her for reasons . . . local, referring to the city of her father's adoption. He had a preconceived idea of what a Kansas City girl was likely to be" (14). It is only after Josephine's manner proves reassuringly genteel and her family history respectable that Bodewin overcomes his skepticism. Related to this "cult of refinement" was the use of dialect to determine one's status. In *John Bodewin's Testimony* the social disparity between the hero and his captors is emphasized by the slang and nonstandard pronunciation of the latter, just as the distance between Josephine and the two miners who gaze at her admiringly is measured by the Irish brogue and the "half breed" silence of the two men.

The tradition of western romance was continued after Cooper by Harte, who in the late 1860s found a congenial content and format. Beginning with "M'lss" and "The Luck of Roaring Camp," Harte focused on the boastful, unreflective qualities of mining life that he encountered in the High Sierras. His tales were anecdotal and avowedly sentimental; they were predicated, in the author's words, on "the existence of a peculiar and romantic state of civilization,"[8] a stage which had passed long before he began writing. Lacking mining knowledge, Harte filled his fiction with character types whose picturesqueness served to compensate for the absence of accurate background detail. His success was such that authors subsequently using mining material were liable to immediate comparison.

In her first two Leadville romances, Foote appropriated Harte's material and gave it new direction, conveying with accuracy the actual business of western mining. *The Led-Horse Claim* and *John Bodewin's Testimony* were followed by a spate of imitators in the 1880s and 1890s, including Robert Louis Stevenson's *The Silverado Squatters* (1883), Enoch More's *Let It Burn* (1892), C. W. Balestier's *Benefits Forgot* (1893), Mrs. H. B. Monroe's *Heroine of a Mining Camp* (1894), and Beveridge Hill's *The Story of a Cañon* (1895). What made these works weaker, in most instances, was the absence of authorial conviction and insufficient knowledge of subject matter; conversely, what came to mark improvement in Foote's work was her growing understanding of the West.

II   *Tales of the Sacrificed Heroine*

The $1,500 Mary received for the serialization of *John Bodewin's Testimony* financed the construction of the Footes' "Stone House,"[9] located some ten miles from Boise in a canyon overlooking the irrigation project; but the house was the only symbol of stability in an increasingly uncertain situation. Their venture had been dealt a damaging blow with the depression of 1884, followed by a sudden and unfavorable change in the project ownership. As a result the work force was reduced to skeletal proportions, with all salaries but Arthur's stopped, and

John and Bessie Sherman were obliged to retreat to Boise, their unsettled situation a source of anguish to the Footes. As Mary observed of her beloved sister and brother-in-law years later in her autobiography: "They had tried riding in our Chariot of Hope, and when neither faith nor works would move it any further, they got out and walked. Brave and sensible people."[10]

It was during this period of anxiety that Mary composed "A Cloud on the Mountain," her first adult tale set in Idaho, publishing it in November 1885. Unnotable otherwise, the unsettling tale of Ruth Mary Tully is clearly a working out of the private fears of Mary Hallock Foote. The story reveals the author's deep concern that her own future, and that of others, is in jeopardy: she renders the unexpected collapse of the eastern financing as the senseless disaster—the fatal cloudburst—that it ultimately proved to be.

The tale deals, like the Babe Keesner chapters of *John Bodewin's Testimony*, with the unrequited love of a young woman for a man of higher rank and with her consequent disillusionment and accident-suicide. In writing the story, Foote may have had in mind Tennyson's "The Princess," which includes the following lines:

> Come down, O maid, from younder mountain height,
> . . . .
> And come, for Love is cf the valley, come,
> For Love is of the valley, come thou down
> And find him . . .
>
> . . . .
> But follow, let the torrent dance thee down
> To find him in the valley. . . . .

Or the inspiration may have been more general, for Ruth Mary's disastrous voyage down a river to see the man she loves reenacts the fates of such Tennysonian heroines as the maiden Elaine and the "Lady of Shalott"—women who languish for a glimpse of a man virtually unaware of their existence, recognize the hopelessness of their love, and deliberately seek a watery bier. Whatever its literary source, the story is the first of Foote's "dark" Idaho tales in which female characters find release in death.

In "A Cloud on the Mountain," the Boise River is transformed into the Bear River, with the low-roofed Tully cabin perched,

like the Idaho Mining and Irrigation engineers' shack, on a cliff
overlooking the river below. In their "tentative home in [the]
solitude of the hills,"[11] the Tully family lives a monotonous
existence. Mrs. Tully is particularly sensitive about the changes
wrought by life in the West: with her "grayish yellow hair of . . .
lifeless texture" and her "limp calico draperies" (152), she is
painfully aware of her reduced circumstances. Ruth Mary, the
Tully's nubile daughter, comes to recognize the narrowness of
their life when a party of mining engineers visits the area. To her
inexperienced eye one of the men, Kirkwood, assumes the
stature of a knight: "He held his fishing-rod, couched like a
lance, in one hand, and a string of gleaming fish in the other"
(161). As Ruth Mary silently experiences the stirrings of first
love, she resolves not to follow the course her family has planned
for her—marriage to her father's younger partner, a packer
named Joe Enselman.

After a brief visit the engineers depart for their claim
downstream, and months pass without Ruth Mary's seeing
Kirkwood again. In the interim, Enselman loses one eye in a
tragic mishap and Ruth Mary—moved by pity and family
pressure—reluctantly agrees to marry him. Though she becomes
betrothed, she does not forget her feelings for Kirkwood; she
secretly "wishe[s] that she were dead. There seemed no way out
of her trouble" (188–89). Fate, in the form of a violent spring
cloudburst, provides the girl a means of escape. Determined to
warn Kirkwood of the impending flash flood, she maneuvers her
boat down the swollen river toward his riverside camp, the
torrent overtaking her just as she reaches her destination. The
uncomprehending Kirkwood, safe with the other men in the
mine, rues the girl's "useless warning" and "passionate sacrifice":
"The pity of it, when he thinks of it sometimes, seems to him
more than he can bear. Yet if Ruth Mary had still been there at
the ranch on the hills, she would have been, to him, only 'that
nice little girl of Tully's who married the one-eyed packer'"
(198).

Foote's choice of "dark" romance—of a melodramatic plot
concluding in death—for "A Cloud on the Mountain" and several
subsequent tales is both predictable and illuminating. Like many
literary artists, she tended to rely most heavily upon romance
during the periods when she was most vulnerable to pessimism.
As V. L. Parrington has noted, romance is "a defense mechanism

against the drab reality": "the greater the disillusion—the more
open roads that end in blind alleys—the greater the need of
prevaricating tenderly about life and the universe, if we are to
keep our poise."[12] During the Idaho period Foote prevaricated
about the universe not by contriving happy endings but by
providing the necessary escapes. Her figures, having renounced
or sacrificed their own happiness to another, find themselves left
to honor an untenable emotional compact. Death becomes
welcome.

In "The Fate of a Voice," Foote's next Idaho fiction, death
occurs only symbolically; the crux of the tale, rather, is the
nature of the heroine's renunciation. The story was written,
Foote told Helena Gilder, "when I was *sick* and disgusted with
myself and everything"; it became another imaginative transmutation of the author's fear that she might be sacrificed to the
Boise scheme. Forced to remain within the confines of the
canyon from April through June of 1886, as the end of her
difficult third pregnancy neared, the thirty-eight-year-old
author blurted out at one point to her best friend, "There *is* no
art for a woman who marries. She may use her gift if she has one,
as a drudge uses her needle, or her broom—but she must be
content to see the soul of it wither and the light of it go out."[13]
That this second Idaho tale is, covertly, a representation of the
author's own psychic stresses becomes evident from its setting
and characterization, as well as from a letter Foote wrote to
Helena in June, just before the birth of her daughter Agnes:

I begin to realize in this time of writing and resting how confused were
the ten years of married life that have gone. What journeys and
anxieties, and vain strivings to adapt myself to near . . . impossible
conditions and all the while the inner experiences of marriage and
motherhood going on—common to most, yet different with each
individual attempt to realize the ideal in the actual.[14]

The discrepancy between the ideal and the actual, between
devotion to art and the East, and loyalty to family and the West,
is developed in the tale through the interplay between Madeline
Hendrie (Molly Hallock) and her older sister. Sallie Duncan
(Mary Foote).

Mrs. Duncan, married to an engineer whose work in the
Wallula River canyon is "temporarily suspended,"[15] welcomes a

summer visit from the talented Madeline, who has been pursuing voice lessons in New York and is to go abroad to complete her training. The story begins at the end of the summer after the pretty visitor has so enlivened the canyon camp with her presence as to capture the heart of Hugh Aldis, one of the engineers. When he proposes marriage, Madeline refuses to accept "the common destiny of woman" (242), insisting that her artistic gifts represent a vocation to which she is already pledged.

On the last evening before she departs, they ascend a bluff overlooking the river and Aldis renews his plea. He argues that Madeline is "blind to a career so much finer, so much broader, so much sweeter, and more womanly," and he insists that no virtue becomes a woman better than renunciation. Madeline remains steadfast, attacking the selfishness of his arguments and explaining that to marry him and live in the West would be to be "buried alive," "mutilated," deprived of expression:

"A beautiful, trained voice is one of the highest products of civilization. . . . It needs the stimulus of refined appreciation. It needs the inspiration of other voices and the spur of intelligent criticism. . . . I won't pretend to depreciate my gift! I am only the tenement in which a precious thing is lodged. You would drive out the divine tenant, or imprison it, for the sake of possessing the poor house it lives in." (230,233)

Their impassioned discussion climaxes when Madeline, insisting they return to camp, trips and loses her footing; Aldis, springing to her rescue, pushes her to safety but plunges over the precipice when the edge of the bluff crumbles. Though his fall is broken and he emerges unhurt, Madeline's fate is more serious: "a shock of the nerves from the sight of his fall . . . deprived her entirely of her voice, so that she could not speak except in whispers" (239).

The accident brings Madeline to a recognition of her love for Aldis at the same time that it accentuates her feelings of guilt and gratitude. Like Ruth Mary, she acquiesces to betrothal by default, for she accepts her loss of voice as just punishment for her "nonsense about Art and Destiny" (246) and agrees to marry Aldis if her voice returns. If it does not, he will be free to break the engagement.

Madeline returns to the East to recover the voice she lost in
the West, and her success is such that she decides to permit
herself one liberty. "The temptation to sing once as she had so
often dreamed of singing, with the support of a magnificent
orchestra; the longing to know just how much she was resigning
in turning her back upon a musical career, were overmastering"
(254). Though her debut is triumphant, her joy vanishes with the
discovery that Aldis, journeying to New York to claim his fiancée,
has arrived prematurely, witnessed the performance, and
renounced his claim to her. Receiving his note of farewell,
Madeline rushes to the train station to explain to him before he
departs, and she is put aboard his train by mistake. Through this
contrived situation the two lovers are reunited as the train roars
westward, and "the fate of a voice" is determined.

Somewhere in that vague and rapidly lessening region known as the
frontier, there disappeared, a few years ago, a woman's voice. . . . She
threw away a charming career, just at its outset, and went West with a
husband—not anybody in particular. . . .
But in the camps of engineers . . . a voice is sometimes heard, . . . a
voice singing in the wilderness, in the dawn of the day of art and beauty
which is coming to a new country and a new people. (274-75)

The tale concludes on a somber note that reinforces the
subdued tone of the work. Madeline is clearly won by default, for
she tells Aldis through her tears, ". . . I am in such trouble!—I
had to see you, after that letter. I ran after the train, and they
caught hold of me and put me on before I knew what they were
doing; and here I am without a ticket or a cent of money" (273).
Though she registers relief upon finding Aldis, there is a
conspicuous absence of joy on her part; it is from *his* point of
view that "the dream [comes] true at last." The final passage of
the story states that Madeline's voice can be heard in the "woods
and the solitudes," but the emphasis is on renunciation and loss:
"the treasured, self-prized gifts are not those that always carry a
blessing with them"; "at all events the voice was lost" (275).
To underscore the fact that the tale is not an unalloyed
celebration of romantic love, Foote subtly inverts the "Lorelei"
legend. According to the version popularized by Heinrich Heine
and Franz Liszt, Lorelei was a beautiful maiden who plunged
into the Rhine in despair over a faithless love. She reemerged as

a siren, dwelling on a high cliff overlooking the river, and wrought her revenge by luring boatmen to destruction with her echoing song. The enchanting and destructive nature of art, "la belle dame sans merci" as victim and victimizer—these elements of the legend are recreated by Foote to demonstrate the incompatibility of love and art. Madeline's "fancy for getting on the brink of things and looking over" brings Aldis to "that fatal place" from which he tumbles (237); before the accident, she bursts into song, "waking from the rocks . . . an echo like the utterance of a voice imprisoned in the cliff" (226). Yet in this crucial episode Foote upsets the reader's expectations by making the traditional seductress the one who is betrayed: "It was not Aldis who was the victim of this tragedy of the bluffs, but Aldis's successful rival, the Voice. It was hushed, at the very moment of its triumph" (239). Later, when Madeline makes her New York debut, she chooses to sing "Die Lorelei," causing Aldis to wonder if she has forgotten their episode on the rocks: "Was this beautiful creature, with eyes alight and soft throat swelling to the notes of her song, merely a voice, after all, celebrating its own triumph and another's allurement and despair?" (261).

The answer, provided by Foote's own experience, is no. For Madeline Hendrie and Molly Hallock, the legend has been turned topsy turvy: the "rare gift" of the artist has itself been lured into destruction—"at all events the voice was lost" (275). The promptings of art have ultimately given way to the more imperious demands of love, with the surrender reflecting the unnatural submission of a superior to an inferior being. Aldis's egotism, which overlooks the fact that but for the accident Madeline would never have pledged herself, is emphasized by his farewell statement in New York: ". . . God knows what sacrifice I might not be base enough to accept, face to face with you again" (267). The nature of that sacrifice, attested to by Madeline's "long, shuddering sobs" as the train onto which she has been thrust hurtles into the West, militates against any interpretation of a happy ending in the fact of their reunion.

The tragedy of Madeline Hendrie, a girl with a "rare gift" torn between the conflicting demands of love and art, is the only "artist" tale Foote ever wrote. Unlike her fellow authors Henry James and Willa Cather, in whose works the plight of the artist is a recurrent theme,[16] she may have found the revelation of her own artistic consciousness too painful—or too immodest. Though she would continue to draw upon her own situation as inspiration for subsequent works, the focus would be her status as woman rather than as artist, with her tales increasingly peopled by heroines who lack control over their destiny.

III *Enforced Idleness*

The pressures under which Mary Hallock Foote lived in 1886 increased during the two subsequent years of waiting for new financing. Life in the canyon was as strained as it was uneventful, with Mary called upon to minister to the concerns of a large household. As she revealed to Helena, the daily demands wore steadily upon her sensitive, solitary nature:

I am daily chopped in little pieces and passed around and devoured and expected to be whole again next day, and all days. And I am *never alone,* for a single minute! . . . I was brought up in a life where, you know, there was plenty of space and long solitary walks and not many people pressing in. It is very hard for my disposition never to have the *room,* inside and out, to breath in.[17]

The tension exacted its toll upon all the principals. Mary's productivity disappeared; she began to suffer from recurrent attacks of neuralgia, a nervous condition characterized by aching and soreness in her face and arms. During 1887 she completed and published only four illustrations and one children's story. Arthur, compelled to seek new eastern backing, was away much of the time, yet his traveling proved an unsuccessful substit′te for the heavy drinking he had begun. His bouts with alcohol became Mary's "great trial in life," the "constant dread" of which she wrote to Helena.[18] Because of Arthur's frequent absences, Mary became increasingly dependent upon twenty-six-year-old Harry Tompkins, her husband's assistant, for emotional support and reassurance. Her close friendship with Tompkins was not without hazards of its own, as she was keenly aware; the handsome young man—in his dual stance of official comforter and unofficial admirer-suitor of the boss's wife—represented for Mary "a great help during the long waiting, as well as a great anxiety."[19]

The next few years proved to be a "close call," as Foote termed it—a fundamental test "in the way of character" of all the canyon inhabitants. Her letters to Helena during this period are surprisingly candid as to the fact that she was confronting many pressures but are less explicit as to their nature. Again and again she recurs to ominous water imagery: the canyon residents are passengers on a "long, long voyage" fraught with the danger of "absolute shipwreck," while the "swift strong current" of the Boise River appears to be "life in the midst of death, no not death, but the lifeless dam of life."[20] Foote's letter of March 6, 1887, to Helena contains a poignant passage which illuminates the personal anguish behind "A Cloud on the Mountain" and "The Fate of a Voice":

These last two years have been the strongest discipline my life has ever known. It is not a thing like sorrow, it is a steady strain and there has been no *limit* fixed—so long we must endure, and then—It has been a hope steadily deferred from day to day—now and then rising—to a climax of certainty—then being dashed down again, to resume the from day to day process.

Nor was Foote insensitive to the emotional toll that the waiting exacted upon Arthur. As she wrote that year in the text to one of her illustrations for "Pictures of the Far West," the frontier "is a world of illusions capable of turning into ordeals":

But occasionally it happens that a man's life pauses in the West, even if he be not altogether "left." The pause may last for months or for years; in the course of it hope and faith in the purpose which brought him there alternate with a sense of absurdity and defeat. . . . [M]others and wives know the peculiar nature of his trial, and pray that he may be remembered in the hour of the march forward, or that he may be loosed from the vow, the enchantment, the delusion—whatever the spell may be that keeps him, dreaming of activity, fast bound in the toils of suspense and enforced idleness.[21]

During this period of intense anxiety, Foote's fiction suffered from her inability to achieve perspective, to disassociate her life from her art. Yet her illustrations reveal a remarkable, positive synthesis of experience and imagination. By the late eighties she had achieved artistic prominence with her character studies and landscapes of the frontier, it generally being agreed that she was the one woman who could "claim company among the men in the field of western picture,"[22] so when Gilder suggested the

Century run a series of full-page drawings of the West during 1888–89, it was Foote who received the commission. Viewing the project as a timely method of release as well as an excellent showcase for her talents, Foote agreed to write brief sketches to accompany the illustrations; as she explained enthusiastically to Gilder, "It will be a great help to get one's personality out of the way."[23]

The resultant "Pictures of the Far West" represents a milestone in Foote's artistic career. The eleven drawings easily rival the best efforts of her illustrator contemporaries and represent a fortuitous matching of subject and sensibility. In mid-1887 Foote had written to Helena of the western landscape she was attempting to capture:

There is something terribly sobering about these solitudes, these waste places of the Earth. They belittle everything one is, or tries to do. The vast wonderful sunsets, the solemn moonlights, and the noise the river makes on dark nights. The wash of water and of land and the immense dignity of it all![24]

It is precisely this dignity and sense of solitude which invest the "Pictures of the Far West" with their staying power. Enthusiastic reviewers praised the series for its breadth of topic and realism in detail, but it took a fellow artist to recognize and articulate the unique harmony between the pictures and their creator. William Allen Rogers, one of the leading western illustrators of the day, offered perhaps the most astute comment on Foote's achievement when he reexamined the "Far West" series and other of her drawings some years later:

If Mrs. Foote were not so identified with her work as a novelist she would be better known as one of the most accomplished illustrators in America. There is a charm about her black-and-white drawing which cannot be described, but it may be accounted for by the fact that, more than any other American illustrator, she lived the pictures from day to day which she drew so sympathetically.

Somehow she and Owen Wister, two products of the most refined culture of the East, got closer to the rough frontier character than any writers I know, and Mrs. Foote supplemented this with pictures that one feels were made while looking from the rim of some deep cañon or by the light of a lantern in a lonesome cabin.[25]

IV The Last Assembly Ball

It was indeed while looking from the rim of the Boise canyon that Foote created "The Pictures of the Far West" and began work on her next project, her first sustained writing since *John Bodewin's Testimony*. Set in Colorado like her two previous novels, *The Last Assembly Ball* (1889) was completed and published in little more than a year. The idea for the story derived from Foote's attendance in Leadville, eleven years earlier, at a "meeting of the 'assembly'—a select . . . ball held in the dining-room of the Clarendon."[26] The memory of the dance gained significance as her perspective on the West matured. Her realization that the gala affair was a means whereby the members preserved their eastern values rather than celebrated their westernness became the impetus for the novel. *The Last Assembly Ball* is a working out of the author's concern about her own deracinated position, about the dangers inherent in a shortsighted allegiance to the East. As Foote wrote to Helena,

[I]t occurred to me that there is a class of Americans not yet classified—strangers in their native land, exiles under their own flag. The relations of these people with other exiles, with the natives they happen to be thrown with, their semi-estrangement from the East, their pride and their despair in the life they lead, their restlessness and their longing for rest, their disaffection and their loyalty seem to me an interesting side of American life. . . . The most bewildering thought is that perhaps we belong to this unclassified class ourselves.[27]

Consisting of only thirteen chapters, Foote's "exile" novel is structured as a three-act tragedy, with the successive acts labeled "The Situation," "The Situation Developed," and "The Catastrophe." The drama centers around twenty-four-year-old Frank Embury, a handsome New York engineer newly arrived in Leadville. Like the master of Tennyson's "Locksley Hall," with whom he is compared in passing, he is seeking adventure in a new region as an antidote to recent disappointment in love. He, too, has pled unsuccessfully for the hand of his cousin—a young girl who, like Tennyson's Amy, has reluctantly acquiesced to her parents' arguments against the marriage. Disconsolate and disgusted, Embury has "hurled himself across the continent by the first train westward."[28] With his partner Hugh Williams, he

gains lodgings in a select boarding house run by the widowed
Mrs. Dansken, who envisions herself as a surrogate parent and
guardian of polite society. She is ever watchful lest young men of
good breeding take the step "so often fatal to Eastern boys":

"Eastern women may be wanted in the West, but Western women are
never wanted in the East. . . . Behave yourselves, my dear boys, and
go home and marry your own girls, to the happiness of all concerned.
And I shall have earned the prayers of your anxious parents." (33–34)

Conscious of the potential temptation represented by a pretty
woman, Mrs. Dansken makes her boarders pledge to remain
aloof from Milly Robinson, a handsome girl she hires as
maidservant.

Embury's susceptibility to beauty, his readiness to redress
wrongs, and his idealism are all sorely tested by Milly's presence.
He attempts to improve her situation by helping her with heavy
chores, engaging her in conversation, and eventually asking her
to the "Assembly" ball. Mrs. Dansken's strenuous objections to
this last action make Embury pity all the more the girl whose
social inadequacy the matron so strongly insists upon. In
sympathetic protest he moves out of the boarding house, buys
Milly an evening gown, and on the eve of the dance impetuously
insists that she wed him, though the consummation of their
marriage is deferred to the morrow. Embury assumes that Milly's
successful debut in society will be assured now that she is his
wife. The drama moves inexorably to disaster as the unwitting
pair arrive at the dance. Williams, in a belated effort to "save"
his friend, has discovered that the girl parading as an innocent
maiden is in reality a widow of unsavory background; this he
makes known to all the Assembly invitees, who mount a united
front against her. It is only after the couple's humiliation at the
dance is complete that Williams, unaware that Embury has
married Milly, tells his partner the secret which has been
revealed to all but him. At first incredulous and then resigned,
Embury engineers his release at the expense of his life. Having
struck a man at the dance in defense of his wife's honor, and
having been subsequently challenged to a duel, he determines to
keep the rendezvous on his wedding night. He welcomes death,
knowing his hasty marriage to be untenable; in the duel he
insures his fate by never firing a shot.

Using her third novel to examine frontier standards of conduct, Foote embellishes her chronicle of the awkward stages of Leadville's social infancy with an introduction:

But as a matter of experience, no society is so puzzling in its relations, so exacting in its demands upon self-restraint, as one which has no methods, which is yet in the stage of fermentation. . . . The life of the West historically, like the story of Man, is an epic, a song tale of grand meanings. Socially, it is a genesis, a formless record of beginnings, tragic, grotesque, sorrowful, unrelated. . . . But looking forward to the story in periods, the West has a future, socially, of enormous promise. It has all the elements of greatness, when it shall have passed the period of uncouth strivings, and that later stage of material satisfaction which is the sequel to the age of force. . . . It has that admixture of contrasting national types which gives us the golden thread of genius. (5-8)

Viewed from the perspective of literary history, what Foote is embracing here is the popular theory of social stages "which places the West below the East in a sequence to which both belong." As Henry Nash Smith has noted, for many nineteenth-century authors utilizing this intellectual framework the prime value recognized was "the refinement which is believed to increase steadily as one moves from primitive simplicity and coarseness toward the complexity and polish of urban life."[29] Thus the severe exclusion of Milly by the Assembly ladies, and Embury's realization that she is not presentable to his mother, are elements which convey Foote's belief that the painful ongoing task of scrutiny and appraisal of its members is a necessary step toward societal maturity.

The Last Assembly Ball deserves notice more for its accurate detailing of Leadville life than for its thematic development, for most aspects of the characterization and plot represent weak variations on its predecessors. Like *The Led-Horse Claim* and *John Bodewin's Testimony,* it depicts the meteoric pattern of life on the mining frontier: fortunes are made and squandered, couples are paired and split asunder, lives flash brilliantly and then flicker out. The descriptions of the chaotic expansion of the mining town, of a claim jumper's funeral, and of life within a makeshift boarding house are excellent, as is the characterization of Mrs. Dansken. But the central details of Foote's "Pseudo-Romance of the Far West"[30] are less convincing. The parallel

between Embury's courtship of Milly and that of the Arthurian
lovers alluded to in the text, Geraint and Enid, is forced. Like
Tennyson's Geraint, Embury woos a lady of broken fortunes; he
bears Milly away, dressed in faded garb like Enid, to be married.
While Geraint later fears that Enid's purity has been endangered
through friendship with the adulterous Guinevere, Embury is
confronted with incontrovertible proof that Milly is not the
maiden she has pretended to be. Taunted by men who slur him,
Embury, like Geraint, suffers shame through his marriage and
regains his self-respect through combat; but unlike the knight of
the Round Table, he pays for this victory with his life.

The Last Assembly Ball is Foote's fourth successive depiction
of death as the result of an untenable emotional compact. In the
earlier instances, it is the heroine, whether avoiding a marriage
or acquiescing to it, who is usually destroyed. In John Bodewin's
Testimony the hero's sister dies in childbirth, achieving a
merciful release from the betrayal and ignominy of her marital
life, while Babe Keesner, facing desertion by Bodewin, seeks out
death. Ruth Mary in "A Cloud on the Mountain" likewise rushes
to her death, escaping marriage with the one-eyed packer, while
Madeline in "The Fate of a Voice" accedes to symbolic death by
accepting a marriage predicated on immurement in the West. In
The Last Assembly Ball this pattern varies slightly: Milly
Robinson, like Ellen Bodewin and Babe Keesner, is also deserted
and betrayed by a lover, but she does not die. It is Frank, the
representative hero, who chooses not to live out a marital lie.
Like Arthur Foote, another engineer of idealistic aspirations, he
has been "endangered by the tragic delusions" (32) of the West;
he too finds escape—not in alcohol, but in a trumped-up duel.

V   Defeat

By March 1889, when The Last Assembly Ball began appearing
serially in the Century, Mary and Arthur were each involved in a
fierce effort to avert disaster. Arthur relinquished the position of
supervisor of the irrigation project after six years of intent
involvement; leaving Tompkins in charge of the active work, he
accepted a position with the U.S. Geological Survey. The move
provided the security of salary as well as the opportunity to
overcome his drinking problem through salutary field work and
exposure to abstemious colleagues whose respect he desired. For

Mary, Arthur's absence signaled a respite from the pressures of the canyon. Moving into John and Bessie Sherman's home in Boise, she evidenced her quiet strength and resourcefulness, taking deliberate steps to assure security for herself and her children. The $1,000 she received for two juvenile "pot-boilers"—works hastily produced for financial gain—went toward enrolling Arthur Burling in an eastern preparatory school and establishing her own financial independence.

In tacit acknowledgment of the precarious state of her marriage, Mary sought haven that summer in Victoria, British Columbia, where, alone with her children, she pondered the uncertain future. That she was considering the possibility of separation is apparent from the veiled references to her "experiment" in letters to Helena; as she explained,

It is so incredible of me to go off like this. Yet it has come upon me like a fate. I feel that we deteriorate in this life of physical inaction and mental unrest. This perpetual rising and sinking upon waves of hope into depths of disappointment wear into the temper into one's very soul. It is too great a price to pay for any scheme.[31]

After three months of deliberation Mary returned to Boise, resolved to stand by her husband. Years later she would gloss over this crucial period in the *Reminiscences,* noting that she was "completely entoiled in the life and temperamental adventures" of her husband and "helpless to direct" her own course. To Helena, however, she was more direct, acknowledging that though she was "irrevocably committed" to Arthur, theirs had become a family "without a future," "without hope."[32]

In 1890, on the strength of new financial backing from the East, work on the irrigation scheme resumed, and Arthur built a family home, the "Mesa House," on flatland near the slowly emerging Boise canal. Arthur was guardedly optimistic about the future; but Mary was "not happy that summer on the Mesa," and her pessimism deepened with the deaths of her mother in August and of her brother-in-law, John Sherman, the following April. Her husband's drinking problem still existed, while the debilitating effects of her own nervous fatigue prevented her from concerted writing; she finished only one story—a juvenile tale—during the year. Intermittently, she worked on the novel she had long wanted to write, "the story of our three summers and two and a half winters in the cañon."[33] It was titled *The Chosen Valley*—and would end with the engineer-hero drowning.

Mary Hallock Foote's premonition that the Idaho campaign would meet with disaster was borne out in 1891 when the eastern investors were forced to foreclose the canal property. This humiliation and disappointment signaled the last of the Footes' agonizing retreats: "We did not leave our bones on that battlefield," Mary later wrote, "but we left pretty much everything else we had. My husband left the crown of his years and the greatest of his hopes, the dream that satisfied the blood of farmers and home-makers in him, and the brain of the constructor he was born to use."[34] Mary and the children moved into the Sherman home, which Bessie had recently converted into a boarding house, while Arthur dedicated himself to untangling irrigation company affairs. During this period it was as if Mary Hallock Foote's life were aping her art *(The Last Assembly Ball)*, with the widow Sherman becoming the widow Dansken and Molly/Milly, the matron-maiden, taking refuge within the boarding house.

Before the disastrous year of 1891 closed, Foote read proof for *The Chosen Valley*, began two children's tales, and published her first adult short story in five years. Judging from her correspondence, this period of renewed production represented not so much a creative resurgence as an act of emotional escape and of financial survival; potboiling became an effective if embarrassing ally. She described the adult tale conceived and published during this period as "an awfully dismal little bore of a story" into which she had worked "I don't know how many fits of the blues."[35] Entitled "The Rapture of Hetty," the account of Jim Basset's abduction of Hetty Rhodes is a modern version of Sir Walter Scott's ballad of the goodly knight "come out of the west."

In Scott's poem *Marmion*, Lochinvar arrives uninvited at the marriage celebration of "the fair Ellen" and Netherby, his rival. Professing to have come "to lead but one measure, drink one cup of wine," Lochinvar claims Ellen in a never-ending dance which leads out the door, onto his steed, and into the night:

> There was racing and chasing, on Cannobie Lee,
> But the lost bride of Netherby ne'er did they see.
> So daring in love, and so dauntless in war,

> Have Ye e'er heard of gallant like young Lochinvar?
>   (*Marmion*, Canto V, Section XII)

"The Rapture of Hetty" alters these elements only slightly. It is a Christmas dance rather than a wedding feast which Jim Basset attends. His love, Hetty Rhodes, is there with his arch rival, a man who, in publicly accusing Basset of cattle thievery, has rendered him a social outcast. Protesting his innocence and his right to attend the dance, Basset offers "in evidence of his good faith and peaceable intentions, to give up his gun; but on the condition that he be allowed one dance with the partner of his choosing, regardless of her previous engagements."[36] The boon is granted: Basset and Hetty circle and circle the room with "the music playing madly," until they plunge out the doorway and are gone.

Foote's tale is escapist romance, as is *Marmion*, but it does not focus solely, as does Scott's poem, on the hero. The emphasis, conveyed by the title, is on Hetty's abduction, on the quiescent heroine being forcefully borne away. In mood the tale recalls "The Fate of a Voice," for neither Madeline Hendrie nor Hetty Rhodes is joyous as she is carried off into the West. Or, viewed from another perspective, the timely arrival of a knightly figure who thwarts the union of the heroine with a lesser man is once again presented ambiguously. In "A Cloud on the Mountain" the appearance of Kirkwood saves Ruth Mary from an unhappy, prearranged marriage but costs her life. In "The Rapture of Hetty" the story concludes on a note of feminine loss rather than masculine triumph:

They crossed the little valley known as Seven Pines; they crashed through the thin ice of the creek; they rode double sixteen miles before daybreak, Hetty wrapped in her lover's "slicker," *with the blue-bordered handkerchief, her only wedding gift, tied over her blowing hair.*(209; italics mine)[37]

The literary value of this slim tale, barely eleven pages in print, is negligible, as Foote was quick to acknowledge. The problem, she knew, lay in her necessity to write quickly and in her inability to detach her fiction from her life. Her Idaho stories were based, at this point, upon seven years of glaringly public financial insecurity and chronic transiency, and upon the concomitant private heartbreaks—Arthur's drinking, Tompkins's infatuation, the Shermans' physical and financial decline. It is no wonder, then, that the fictions reflected a strange intermingling of romantic escapism and grim realism, and that they concluded ambiguously. As 1891 closed, Mary Hallock Foote exclaimed to Richard Watson Gilder, "I do so hope I shall not fall below the standard of the magazine! I have it always in mind as a nightmare, for I am less and less capable of judging my own work, I find. I suppose it is getting too familiar with the life I try to write about. . . . I wish I could get away from it."[38] It would be four more years before she could begin to distance her life from her art.

CHAPTER 4

Experimentation

I   The Chosen Valley

DURING 1892, while the Footes continued to board at Bessie's, Mary was engaged in completing *The Chosen Valley* and Arthur was involved in a new but considerably more modest irrigation venture. As Mary confided to Helena in a burst of bitterness:

> These schemes are all the very D---- for forcing a man off his balance, and mixing up his estimates of the relative value of things. Our canal is a perfect Frankenstein; it has a sort of life of its own and carries us along in tow. It amounts to a fate for this family.[1]

Once again Mary Hallock Foote's premonitions of disaster proved founded. As she later explained, wryly, in the *Reminiscences,* Arthur "had located a reservoir site at a place in the [Idaho] backlands called Ten Mile or Indian Creek." Approached by an engineer-promoter representing an eastern investor, he had been asked "to name his price. The work itself was all A. asked—to build his own dam, on the salary of a chief engineer." On the strength of a verbal agreement, Arthur had divulged his maps and drawings and the engineer-promoter had departed, ostensibly to report to his investor in the East. Some time later it became clear that Arthur's claim had been jumped and recorded in the name of the investor, while the engineer who had masterminded the swindle took charge of completing the scheme. In Mary's words, the engineer "took A.'s idea for the dam and left out the essential feature, the 'core walls,' and the dam went out before the reservoir was half full. . . . This was the last piece of property of the imagination left him [Arthur] in Idaho that could be lost or stolen."[2]

Altering and incorporating the germ of this humiliating episode into her novel, Foote completed *The Chosen Valley* quickly, as if in hopes of exorcising the family Frankenstein by writing about it. She had begun the novel, provisionally entitled "The History of a Scheme" or "The Waters of Meribah," intending it to be "the story of our *doings*, day by day." As the tale progressed, she became alarmed lest its transparency become an embarrassment to those concerned. At one point she even warned her editors, "I am rather nervous over a way the events of our own scheme have of startling me . . . with an unexpected likeness to my own overdue tale."[3] Her worries were allayed, however, by the favorable reception accorded the novel by critics and readers alike. As she wrote Helena with genuine surprise, *The Chosen Valley* seemed "to remind everybody of some scheme of their own."[4]

Although the novel begins and ends with one Philip Norrison, it is actually the story of Robert Dunsmuir, for it is he whose relations with the other characters generate the crucial conflicts upon which the tale is based. A conscientious Scottish engineer, he had originally been partner in a Snake River irrigation venture with Price Norrison, a ruthlessly practical and mercenary American businessman. When Norrison insisted that a canal dam had to be completed rapidly, regardless of structural soundness, Dunsmuir withdrew from the project, retaining, however, his valuable water rights downstream. The central events unfold ten years later when Norrison, having completed one dam, is attempting to "freeze out" Dunsmuir. Convinced that the Scotsman now has no recourse but to relinquish his water rights, Norrison calls on his engineer son Philip to help him complete a second dam. As father explains to son, "Dunsmuir has been laughed at and called a crank these ten years; but people have got used to thinking of him, holding on with a bulldog grip, staking every penny he's got on the game, and year after year of his life—not to speak of the lives of his wife and children."[5]

Much to Norrison's chagrin, Philip develops a strong admiration for the scruples of Dunsmuir and a corresponding distaste for his own father's worship of expediency. At the same time Dunsmuir's son, Alan, defects to seek employment from Norrison, and Philip falls in love with Dunsmuir's daughter, Dolly. Thus the engineer finds himself embattled on all sides: his son has become disaffected; his erstwhile partner turned rival is pressuring him to surrender his water rights or join the project; and his new ally is seeking the hand of his only daughter. The only disinterested friends on whom he can rely are Job and Margaret, the couple who have served him faithfully for years and are regarded as part of the family.

Harboring grave reservations, Dunsmuir at last accedes to becoming chief engineer for the dam project; he has "worn out his powers of waiting" (235). Against his objections, Norrison orders that construction be completed with an eye to profit rather than design; the day before the official opening, the dam collapses. Those who lose their lives are the "two most closely bound up in the history of the work" (308)—Dunsmuir and Job. Their deaths—added to that of Mrs. Dunsmuir, who had been "sacrificed" to the scheme long before—are only slightly propitiated by the subsequent rebuilding and dedication of the dam to Dunsmuir, and by the marriage of Philip and Dolly. As Foote observes in the final paragraph of the novel:

Over the graves of the dead, and over the hearts of the living, presses the cruel expansion of our country's material progress: the prophets are confounded, the promise withdrawn, the people imagine a vain thing. . . . And those that are with it in its latter days are not those who set out in the beginning. And victory, if it come, shall border hard upon defeat. (314)

Foote told a reviewer that the character of Dunsmuir, "a composite of reflected personalities," was based in part on Charles H. Burt, a distinguished Scottish engraver with whom she had worked in New York City.[6] But more to the point is the identification of Dunsmuir with Arthur, for *The Chosen Valley* is clearly Mary's valedictory to the Idaho Mining and Irrigation venture. Dunsmuir, whose scheme is "in advance of its time," lives, like Arthur, in a stone house in the Boise canyon. Supported by the faithful Job and Margaret (John and Bessie Sherman) yet bereft of wifely support, he is one of those men whose "persistence was the despair of their families and the ruin of their fortunes" (54). Seemingly defeated by his project, he ultimately achieves recognition when the newly rebuilt dam is dedicated to his memory. Prophetically, Arthur would receive, eighteen years after the financial collapse of his project, similar recognition upon the completion of the Boise canal.[7]

By contrasting the generation of Robert Dunsmuir and his late

wife with that represented by Philip and Dolly, Foote is
measuring the present fortunes of Arthur and Mary against the
promise they represented in the past. Philip is the same
engineer-hero as Hilgard, Bodewin, and Embury: he is young,
handsome, well educated, attracted to the West. His love
interest, again following the Foote formula, is the daughter of a
rival family. Like Molly Hallock, Dolly Dunsmuir comes from a
"proud, poky family" that mixes little with its neighbors; she too
longs for the old home, the place of her birth, but fears she will
no longer fit in. The other major figure, symbolically named *Price*
Norrison, is a composite of all the eastern businessmen—
including the Indian Creek promoter—whose concern with
immediate profit undermined Arthur's visions and reflected "the
meddlesome impatience of little-minded men."

Just before the novel began to appear serially, Foote had
observed to Gilder apropos one of her earlier tales, "My work is a
helplessly faithful rendering into fiction of the experiences (my
own and those of others) that have come under my own
observation. It will only grow strong and varied as I grow, or
don't grow."[8] *The Chosen Valley* evidences her growth, for it
represents a marked advance over its predecessors in matters of
treatment as well as theme. Foote's portrait of the relationship
between Dunsmuir and Margaret is particularly good: the
Scottish dialect of both characters is skillfully rendered, the
depiction of their mutual respect is convincing, and their final
conversational exchange is poignant and memorable. Also
worthy of note is Foote's use of biblical allusions to enhance the
reader's understanding of the central conflict. Norrison, early
pictured as "the Moses of emigration . . . even to the smiting of
the dry hills to furnish forth water for the reclamation of the
land" (8), is shown to be a false prophet, with Dunsmuir finally
the true Moses. In bringing forth the water Dunsmuir com-
promises his principles, as Moses did at Meribah, and is not
allowed to see the culmination of his lifelong endeavor. He dies,
recognizing that "the work as I planned it remains for some other
man to do" (297). Norrison and Dunsmuir are also likened to
Jacob and Esau, the latter being, in Foote's version, the man who
is "first broken and then bought" (311).

The Chosen Valley depends more upon dialogue, less upon
narrative, than any of Foote's earlier novels except *The Last
Assembly Ball;* to use Henry James's terminology, the shift is

from "picture" to "scene." This technique of depicting the actual moment is a difficult one which, when handled well, invests the novel with the immediacy of drama. Occasionally, however, the dramatic potential is vitiated by stilted interviews between lovers or by the extended passages of apologia which derive from two thematic weaknesses of the novel—the twice-developed narrative of the dam dispute and the implausible subplot involving the younger Dunsmuir's desertion of his father.

In her earlier Colorado novels Foote had written of the life around her by emphasizing its western "difference" rather than by examining its essence, but in *The Chosen Valley* her intimate familiarity with the locale and her vested interest in the very subject about which she writes enable her to handle her materials with sympathy and authority. The resultant spirit of honesty and authenticity places the novel within the prevailing literary tradition of the period, that of "local color."

The term "local color," sometimes used to refer to any imaginative writing that partakes of a particular locale, had a more precise meaning for Foote and other writers at the turn of the century. It signified literature in which locale was always a vital, if not central, factor in the reader's interest, and it referred to the narrowly local rather than the regional or sectional. The emphasis was on details which differentiated a specific place from all others. As W. D. Howells proclaimed in one of his literary editorials,"[F]or all aesthetic purposes the American people are not a nation, but a condition. We for our part do not believe that the novel of the United States ever will be, or ever can be, written, . . . [T]here can be no national American fiction, but only provincial, only parochial fictions evermore."[9]

The first generation of local colorists—those writing their major works between, roughly, 1870 and 1890—included Harriet Beecher Stowe, Edward Eggleston, Bret Harte, George Washington Cable, and Sarah Orne Jewett among countless others. For the serious artists, the genre prescribed not only a characteristic organization of subject matter but also a point of view imposed by cultural necessity. The stories placed great emphasis on the climate, resources, period, cultural traditions, and racial or religious heritage of the inhabitants. Plot was deemphasized in favor of setting; characters were almost always "simple" people, but whether they could be characterized as "ordinary" depended upon one's vantage point. To those living

outside the locale depicted, the characters often seemed unusual
or eccentric.

The second generation of local colorists altered the emphasis
of the movement but retained its essence. Led by Hamlin
Garland, Mary Noilles Murfree, Kate Chopin, and Mary E.
Wilkins Freeman, authors were truly awakened to the potential
effects of setting upon human character. Garland's application of
the theories of Spencer and Taine to literature led to the
increasing emphasis on physical background as a conditioning
factor, though the local colorists stopped short of Darwinian
naturalism. "Local color—what is it?" Garland asked
rhetorically: "It means that the writer spontaneously reflects the
life which goes on around him. It is natural and unstrained
art. . . . *Local color in a novel means that it has such quality of
texture and back-ground that it could not have been written in
any other place or by any one else than a native.*"[10]

As a local-color novel, *The Chosen Valley* falls short of
Garland's dicta and of the mark set by *Main-Travelled Roads,
The Country of the Pointed Firs,* and *Before the Gringo Came*—
other such works published during the early and mid 1890s. But
Foote's theme and setting are original, her characterization
unswerving, and her emphasis on the manners of the longtime
residents marks an increased awareness of the potential of locale.
As the first novel based on an area she knew thoroughly, it marks
a significant departure from her earlier romances and serves as
prelude to the best of her later works.

II   *"Quick Sales"*

By the time *The Chosen Valley* appeared in print, Foote's
spirits were somewhat improved. Arthur's acceptance of a
mining position in Baja California had temporarily assuaged their
gnawing uncertainty over his professional future. As Foote
explained with defensive pride to Mary Hague,

You must remember your brother Arthur has *not* made a failure here,
in the sense that there is anything against him, either professionally or
against his character. . . . [A]nd you must not for one moment think
that your brother Arthur amounts to nothing because he is not making
money. He is making character, and is a better comrade and a tenderer,
deeper, stronger man for his trials. It is only fine natures that can rise

through bitter disappointment and unsuccess; and I have seen my husband progress grimly, in patience and silence, through bitter trials; and speaking as an outsider might speak I can say I have never admired him more than I have this past year.[11]

To Helena she wrote less guardedly, happily confiding that Arthur had "gained the mastery" over drinking. Though Foote's assessment proved overly optimistic,[12] the next three years did bring a respite from "illnesses" for her husband in California and for herself in Idaho; moreover, the period brought Mary Hallock Foote unexpected professional rewards.

Recognition of her accomplishments as an illustrator came in the form of an invitation to serve as an Art Juror at the Columbian Exposition (Chicago World's Fair, 1893). Pleased by her selection but concerned by her mistaken appointment to the awards jury for etching rather than black-and-white, Mary Hallock Foote discharged her duties at Chicago with mixed feelings, explaining to Helena afterward,

I was very sick at heart and half defiant as one must be not to be crushed; it is one reason why I am not happy among Artists; I'm just enough like them to feel the differences keenly.

Art is my stern, ironical taskmistress and she calls me a fool whenever I do my best; but I have to go on. It did hurt and humiliate me to have those Artists think that I called myself an Artist.[13]

Neither artists nor critics shared Mary Hallock Foote's misgivings about her talent. Her alma mater, the Cooper Union School of Design, sought her for the principalship. The *Century* initiated its "Series of American Artists" in 1893 with Foote as the lead figure, and in 1894 Alpheus Cody could proclaim without dispute that Foote was "the best known woman illustrator in America."[14] With election to the National Academy of Women Painters and Sculptors, her position as the "dean of women illustrators" was assured.

New acclaim was also accorded to Foote as a writer. During the early 1890s the Winchester Repeating Arms Company honored her, owning the importance it attached to "the frequent allusion to the Winchester rifle" in her work; C. W. Balestier implicitly acknowledged his literary debt to her with his novel *Benefits Forgot*[15]; other literary monthlies increasingly requested the fiction she usually guaranteed the *Century;* and a meaningful and longlived correspondence with Rudyard Kipling began. Moreover, in the space of less than three years, she saw through the press another novel, five adult tales, two juvenile stories, and two collections of her shorter works.

The sudden resurgence of Mary Hallock Foote's career is explained, to a great extent, by resourcefulness born of economic necessity. Freed from the anxieties of the irrigation venture, she faced, in her mid-forties, the significant challenge of providing the sole family income. Potboiling again became her metier. "I look back to that third-story bedroom at Bessie's, where my writing was done, as the best place for the purpose I have ever known," she later reminisced,

and my work in that room was blessed, if it be blessed to "sell"—I am not so sure about that! The themes were the best that ever came to me, but if they had been returned and kept for ten years till they had ripened and settled on their lees, I might have poured a purer wine. But quick sales were very needful at that time.[16]

That the quality of her work often suffered during this period is particularly evidenced by a short story she saw through the press late in 1893, when the California bank in which Arthur had been depositing his irregular Baja earnings collapsed during the national panic. "The Watchman," as the piece is titled, bears a kinship to *The Chosen Valley,* for it was originally drafted during the same period and reflects the same theme of a western irrigation conflict between resident claimants and outside investors. Unlike the novel, however, the tale suffers from a paucity of imagination; Foote even apologized to her editors for having to make it "count for as much as it will."[17]

The story recounts the trials of Travis, a conscientious young man hired by an eastern company to patrol its irrigation ditch. Despite his diligence, mysterious breaks occur with infuriating regularity along the portion of the canal under his charge. His steadfastness in the face of calamity earns him the admiration of Nancy Lark, a resident of the area, until the day Travis catches her father engaged in clandestine hole digging activities. Protesting her father's innocence, Nancy rallies to his defense. The younger man's humiliation is complete when, having had to detect and mend Lark's holes, he is later held responsible when

the ditch wall collapses and the surrounding farms are washed
out. After Nancy, stricken by remorse, acknowledges her father's
culpability, Travis's fortunes rise. Mr. Lark's opposition to the
ditch is silenced by his death, Travis and Nancy are reconciled
and married, and the company ultimately reinstates its
scrupulous watchman.

This "Ditch pastoral,"[18] as Foote once referred to it, reads
more like a juvenile tale than an adult story: the diction is simple,
the plot uninspired, the characterization one-dimensional. While
the affair between the watchman and the girl follows the
Capulet-Montague progression of Foote's earlier fictions, most
notably *The Chosen Valley*, it lacks the supporting rationale and
background. Travis, like Philip Norrison, is described as one of
the "clever sons of Jacob," and Nancy, like Dolly Dunsmuir, is
the "daughter of Esau." Yet this opposition is muted, achieving
explicit statement only once in the story:

Nancy felt bitterly the insignificance of such small scattered folk as her
father, pitiful even in their spite. Their vengeance was like the malice
of field-mice or rabbits, which the farmers fenced out of their fields
into the desert where they belonged. What could such as they do either
to help or hinder this invincible march of capital into the country
where they, with untold hardships, had located the first claims?[19]

"The Watchman," which might have benefited from "ten years'
ripening and settling," is the weakest of the magazine stories
which Foote chose to reprint in 1894. Along with "Friend
Barton's 'Concern,'" "The Story of the Alcázar," "A Cloud on
the Mountain," and "The Rapture of Hetty," it appeared with
the title story in her volume *In Exile, and Other Stories*. The
collection proved uneven, owing to the thin, hastily written
Idaho stories; only the three early productions redeem the
volume from mediocrity.

III   Coeur d'Alene

In 1887 Mary Hallock Foote had written to Helena, "It does
not seem as if an artist should become an 'organ,' though I
suppose artists, especially the old ones, were great fighters for
their own creeds"; five years later, however, she found herself
waging a literary battle to vindicate the integrity and authority
of mining management. Stirred by reports of a violent mining

strike which had erupted in Idaho's Coeur d'Alene district, she
enlisted her pen to make an outcry. Whether the strike was
justified was, Foote explained to her editors at the *Century*, "the
burning question in every mining community of the West—and in
camp after camp it has to be fought out."[20] In *Coeur d'Alene*,
serialized in the *Century* from February to May of 1894 and
published as a book later that year, she restaged the controver-
sial labor-capital war, portraying the deplorable behavior of
union members and emphasizing the reasonableness of the mine
owners. When the *Century* voiced concern over the potential
libel problems involved in publication, Foote responded un-
swervingly, "It is so seldom one gets such a chance as this to call a
spade a spade."[21]

According to modern scholarship, what occurred in Idaho's
northern panhandle in 1892 was the logical outgrowth of a
complex, highly sensitive dispute. Until the late 1880s the silver
and lead mines in the Coeur d'Alene district had not unionized,
but their employees were paid by area mine owners at a rate
established by the Butte Miners' Union in 1878: $3.50 per ten-
hour day for work underground (miners) and for carmen and
shovelers (muckers). When Coeur d'Alene mine owners reduced
these rates by 50 cents in 1887, the laborers began to form local
unions. According to a study by Robert W. Smith, the "mainte-
nance of high wages, the breaking down of the corporation's
commercial monopoly, the protection of life and limb while on
the job, the proper care of sick and injured, and the decent burial
of the dead—these were the ideals of miners' unionism and the
mainsprings of union activity."[22] Miners' pay returned to $3.50 a
day but muckers' remained at $3.00 a day. In January 1891 the
first contest between labor and capital took place. Concerned
that the recent introduction of compressed air drills had
displaced many miners and forced others to become muckers,
the union members rewrote their constitution so that all mine
workers could belong, and then asked for a universal wage scale
of $3.50. A strike action successfully overcame the protests of
mine management, and the mines reopened under the new wage
agreement.

The mine owners and management promptly formed the Mine
Owners' Protective Association (MOA) in February 1891. The
group cited concern over the prevailing low metal rates, high
transportation costs, and high labor wages. The avowed objec-

tives of the MOA were "cooperation in dealing with the railroads over freight rates, cooperation in effecting economies in the operation of mines and mills, and cooperation in dealing with the miners' unions."[23] In January of 1892, after the railroads would not rescind a recent rate raise of $2 a ton on ores transported to smelters, the MOA closed the Coeur d'Alene mines, "preferring to keep their ore reserves undepleted than work their mines with inadequate profits." In March, the MOA announced the railroads' rescission of the rate increase and called for the resumption of mining by April; underground miners would receive $3.50 a day; all others, $3.00. When the union, protesting this reversion to the old rates, refused to work, the MOA responded with a lock-out of union members. Beginning in late April, nonunion labor was imported into the district, and once union harrassment of the "scabs" occurred, the MOA won court injunctions against union interference.

By July feelings ran high among the 700 union members still in the area despite six months of unemployment; they felt the crucial issue was whether the miners' union would continue to exist as a wage bargaining agent. On July 9 the discovery within their ranks of a Pinkerton detective, hired as a spy by the MOA, ignited the violence. On the two succeeding days nonunion men were assaulted, the Frisco Mill dynamited, and valuable mine property seized. The surrender of the mine owners was purchased at the cost of six men's lives. On July 11 approximately 130 nonunion men and a few women and children were escorted out of the district under union guard to a boat landing, from which they were to catch a steamer to Washington. But the deportation did not prove peaceable; a group of eight to twelve armed robbers appeared that evening, marauding the waiting group and terrifying it with threatened violence. When word of the event reached Boise the next day, mass murder on the part of the union was alleged and the Governor proclaimed martial law. Although the surprise attack was later shown to have resulted in widespread robbery but no known deaths, the union was held accountable for the "mission massacre" and the preceding violence at the mines. Eventually both capital and labor claimed hollow victories in the costly war of 1892. The mines boasted of reopening at the old rates and with nonunion labor; the Coeur d'Alene unions regained stature when most of their members brought to trial were acquitted.

As she read the newspapers and received reports from W. B. Heyburn, chief legal counsel for the MOA, during the fall of 1892, Mary Hallock Foote determined to fashion a realistic chronicle of the affair.[24] Like Stephen Crane, who in 1895 would publish a vivid account of war solely from secondary sources, Foote was able to convey the reality of a physical conflict she had not witnessed. Goaded by indignation, however, she substituted spirit and force for detached reporting—as when she graphically depicted murder as well as robbery in the climactic mission scene. The later reports of lack of evidence to substantiate murder did not weaken her personal belief that a massacre had indeed occurred.

The plot of *Coeur d'Alene* is straightforward, with the detailed presentation of the mining dispute eventually upstaging the central love story. Darcie Hamilton, son of one of the British directors of the Big Horn mine, travels incognito to make a secret investigation of the financially troubled Big Horn. Assuming the alias of "Jack Darcie" and the role of partner to Mike McGowan, an independent prospector, Darcie discovers the mine to be ineptly managed by the alcoholic Mr. Bingham, whose prounion sympathies coupled with unscrupulous economic practices represent a dangerous combination. Darcie prepares a report recommending that the mine be shut down; but before mailing it, he meets Bingham's daughter Faith, with whom he falls in love. Keenly aware of the conflict between his duty to inform on Bingham and his desire to win the love of Bingham's daughter, he wavers between reporting his findings to the Board and submitting his resignation. His hesitation proves costly, for his union enemies resort to wounding him and confiscating his unmailed report.

Faith's disgust with her father's inebriation and sympathy for Darcie bring her close to acknowledging her love, but she is stunned by the miners' announcement that Darcie is a spy. As the friction between union and nonunion factions mounts, Faith realizes that her continued presence in the Coeur d'Alene is untenable; she stays just long enough to witness the demolition of the Frisco Mill by the striking miners, the managers' surrender of the Gem mine, and the total collapse of the old order. When the victorious union forces arrange for a train bearing the captive nonunion contingent to depart the strife-torn area, Faith joins the men and women aboard, hoping that Darcie and Mike will be

able to elude the strikers and meet her at the landing. Before
arriving at the mission landing, however, she learns from a union
sympathizer that the union does not intend to surrender its
prisoners alive. When Darcie and Mike reach the mission
vicinity, she warns them of the impending massacre, but Darcie's
recent wound renders him incapable of further flight. By hiding
in the grass the three escape the butchery and robbery around
them and are rescued by federal troops. A few months later the
love affair, forced by the hothouse atmosphere of strife, reaches
full bloom: Darcie marries Faith and assumes the management of
the Big Horn.

In certain respects, the formulaic pattern of *Coeur d'Alene*
resembles that of Foote's earlier Colorado romances. The love
affair is, as one reviewer observed, between "the same
exasperatingly lovely virgin and adventuresome youth" who
always people Foote's stories and who always belong to rival
factions.[25] As in *The Led-Horse Claim,* a trusted physician and a
mining associate befriend the non-western hero, while the
motherless, eastern heroine is betrayed by the alcoholic
deterioration of her closest relative in the West. There follows
also the earlier pattern of a lovers' tryst and of the heroine's
ministering to the hero's convalescence. Similarly, whereas in
John Bodewin's Testimony the hero is torn between his debt to
the villain, who urges him to keep an unholy silence, and his love
for the heroine, who asks that he speak for the cause of justice, in
Coeur d'Alene the hero's dilemma is whether to maintain an
unholy silence for the heroine's sake.

From a broader perspective, however, it becomes evident that
Foote resorted to the romance form only as a convenient vehicle
from which to mount her polemical assault. As she explained to
C. C. Buel of the *Century* when she submitted the first part of
her manuscript, the work had originally been conceived and
drafted as a play: "What you have now [chapters I-IX] was, as I
first wrote it, the first 3 acts. That will explain why I have so
forced the effects. It is not fine or subtle but I was not aiming for
that. I wanted it to go with a rush."[26] Thus in Foote's tale of
Darcie and Faith, as in the parallel Hawthorne tale of Goodman
Brown and Faith, the presentation of the heroine's trust which
turns to doubt and of the hero's attempt to regain that faith is less
powerful than the revelation of a darker evil. In "Young
Goodman Brown" the evil is a witches' sabbath; in Foote's

version, the devilish compact is the miners' union:

Not the least among the hardships of the peaceable, frugal, and laborious poor it is to endure the tyranny of mobs, who with lawless force dictate to them, under penalty of peril to limb and life, where, when, and upon what terms they may earn a livelihood for themselves and their families.[27]

To underscore this point, Foote embroiders historical fact by fabricating the murder of a mining boss by a union member and portraying the death of a harrassed "scab." Several reviewers praised such elements as forceful; others considered the work marred by bitterness.

Though the Coeur d'Alene strike of 1892 passed into history, interest in Foote's account continued into the twentieth century. The novel, which had originated as a play, was subsequently dramatized and was also serialized by a newspaper.[28] To modern tastes, the love story is strained and colorless and the antiunion sentiment outmoded, but the horror of the mission massacre remains utterly convincing. In the use of a topical theme and strident tone, *Coeur d'Alene* is unique among Foote's writings; it is a work of propaganda, born of genuine outrage. "It was the most cowardly brutal thing ever heard of," Foote declared of the "massacre,"[29] and she presented it in just that light.

IV   The Cup of Trembling

Following the appearance of *Coeur d'Alene,* Foote collected for book publication four tales written between 1892 and 1894. Just as the stories of *In Exile* had revealed the author's uncertainty over her provisional status in the West, so this second volume, *The Cup of Trembling, and Other Stories* (1895), captures the anguish of the critical Idaho years. For those most intimately associated with it, the collapse of the irrigation project had been a devastating blow. For Arthur it had brought the ignominy of defeat and the humiliation of having to reestablish his credentials in the profession he entered so long before. For Tompkins, nominal head of the project after 1889, it had signaled the end of a complex relationship with the Footes which proved both gratifying and frustrating. For Mary, it had meant desperate reliance upon writing as a means of livelihood, and the departure of those on whom she most depended for emotional support. In her first extended Idaho fiction, *The Chosen Valley*, Foote had voiced, through the comments of Dolly Dunsmuir, her own sentiments about close canyon living: "[T]here is something deadening in the sight of these bluffs that never change, and these lights and winds and sounds that go from year to year. I wonder we are not all a little touched. I think we are a wee bit off, each one of us in a way of our own."[30] The state of being "off," of deviating from the course prescribed by social convention, is the condition Foote explores in *The Cup of Trembling* through the presentation in each tale of an unorthodox love affair. In "On a Side-Track," the first of the stories in order of composition,[31] this situation is emphasized by a railway metaphor: the hero and heroine are snowbound in a railroad car which is not on the main track. The subsequent stories develop the theme more directly: each heroine transgresses the bounds of propriety, losing her lover's affections and paying with her life.

In "On a Side-Track" Phebe Underhill, an eastern Quaker traveling westward with her father on the Oregon Shortline, arouses the interest of a fellow passenger, Charles Ludovic. Though the girl is unconscious of her charms, the young man appreciates her delicate roselike beauty. Capitalizing on the frequent absence of Phebe's father due to illness, Ludovic pays court to her; when the train becomes snowbound in Idaho for two days, he presses her to pledge her affections. It is only as the reinstated train nears the youth's destination that he admits he is not the free, straightforward man he appears; rather, he is in a predicament resulting from "that union of good blood with hard conditions so often seen in the old-young graduates of the life schools of the West."[32] He explains that he is returning to Pocatello under armed escort to stand trial for the shooting of a man some days before. In spite of his uncertain future, Ludovic selfishly makes a final appeal for Phebe's sympathy; it is, as one reviewer aptly commented, "the grimmest wooing since Richard won the Lady Anne." Ludovic marries Phebe after the Idaho jury rules the murder to have been self-defense, but the issue of their future happiness is left to speculation: "The case is in her hands now. She may punish, she may avenge, as she will, for Ludovic is the slave of his own remorseless conquest. But Phebe has never discovered that she was wronged" (173).

"Maverick," the second tale, is a somber variation on "Beauty and the Beast." In the French fairy tale, Beauty, who imperils her life because of a rose taken from Beast's garden, has the good sense, ultimately, to prefer virtue to wit or beauty. She accepts Beast's proposal of marriage and discovers him to be a prince. Foote's heroine is neither as clever nor as fortunate; her fate is similar to that of Beauty's sisters, whom Beast turns to stone. As a resident of an isolated stage-station in Idaho, Rose Gilroy chafes under her enforced isolation. There are no suitable female companions nearby, and the scenic resources of the area are equally bleak: black lava fields border the town and extend, like a "Plutonian gulf," for 100 miles toward the Snake River. Against this backdrop Rose is observed by a college student, who happens to be passing through and who serves as the story's narrator. He notes that the girl moves restively under the affectionate gaze of Maverick, the local sheriff, whose early Indian captivity left his face grotesquely disfigured. Seeking to escape her repugnant suitor, Rose elopes with a Swedish waiter from the station inn; she disguises herself as a man and the pair flee under cover of night. The sheriff, with the unwitting student at his side, rides in pursuit and shoots the Swede when the latter fires on him. Maverick insists that the girl return to town with him, but she recoils: "She was a rose, but a rose that had been trampled in the dust; and her prayer was to be left there, rather than that we should take her home" (109). Maverick's steadfastness forces Rose at last to choose the only alternative: she eludes her escort during the night and flees, on foot, to certain death in the stony lava fields.

"The Trumpeter," completed and published in 1894, shares with its companion tales an Idaho setting and a flowerlike heroine. Meta is a beautiful halfbreed adopted by the Meadows family of Bisuka (Boise). Callie Meadows, closest in age to the Indian girl, treats her with sisterly kindness until Meta steals the attentions of her fiancé, the trumpeter of the local cavalry troop. Callie mourns her loss but masters her emotions, while Meta proves as impure as her bloodline; she is likened to a mariposa lily, "mooned at the base with a dark, purplish stain which masks the flower with startling beauty, yet to some eyes seems to mar it as well" (182). Meta's love affair and secret marriage to Henniker, the trumpeter, remain unknown until, months after the troops have been reassigned, her pregnant state cannot be ignored. Resolving to escape her ignominious situation by joining her husband, the girl relies upon Indian shrewdness and sheer willpower to withstand the arduous trip from southern Idaho to Montana. As she nears her husband's post at last, Henniker flashes past on a stagecoach bound for town. Although he recognizes as his wife the dirty foottraveler dressed in Indian garb and clutching a child, he is too proud to acknowledge her. After Meta dies on the road, Henniker's friends realize the extent of his shallowness. Like his late wife, the trumpeter loses caste with his friends and determines to flee.

For several years Henniker leads a life of poverty and dissipation which culminates in his joining the Idaho branch of "Coxey's army." He becomes part of what Foote, who saw the group in Boise in 1894,[33] characterizes as a "mob bullying and begging its way eastward" (248). When the Coxeyites are corralled in army camps near Bisuka, Henniker begins to comprehend the extent of his decline. He catches glimpses of Callie, affianced to another military man; of Mrs. Meadows, who refuses his entreaties; and of his son Ross, who remains blissfully unaware that the person he considers a lame "dirty, old man" is his father. Humiliated and aggrieved, Henniker seeks escape by drowning, vowing, "The next time I'm inspected . . . I shall be a clean man" (273).

The last of the short Idaho fictions Foote wrote, "The Cup of Trembling" is the most arresting and the most finished story of the collection. Its theme of elopement and death is presented so directly and forcibly that the author first thought of writing it anonymously. Yet ultimately she signed her name to the manuscript and submitted it to the *Century* with a defensive note:

I am sending you a story which I'm afraid you will say won't do; but please don't say it till you've read it through. I know it's an ugly theme, but it would have to come in once, at least, in any true series of western tales. . . . I think it a moral tale, myself—and I'm not afraid but you will—but of course you know your "general reader."[34]

The heroine of the tale is the beautiful Esmée, an easterner come to the West as a bride. Bound by vows to a life that is "all a pretense and a lie," she regrets her marriage to one of the richest mine owners in the Coeur d'Alene; he strikes her now as a

"rough Western man" made common by the environment.
Reawakened to the possibilities of love by Jack Waring, a
sensitive engineer serving as superintendent to her husband,
Esmée consents to elope with him to his mountain mine, the
Dreadnaught. For several days the pair, snowbound during the
fierce Idaho winter, experience the joys and fears of their
"ridiculous, blissful, squalid" situation. For Esmée, the shock of
adjustment is particularly keen: "She had never before lived in a
house where the fires went out at night, and water froze beside
her bed, and the floors were carpetless and cold as the world's
indifference to her fate" (25).

The crisis for the two lovers comes not with the return of
Esmée's husband, who is out of the state on business, but with the
unexpected appearance of Jack's brother. Invited months earlier
to visit, he arrives as unprepared for the rough weather as for
Jack's altered situation. During a lull in the storm he makes his
way to the mountain cabin, only to be refused entrance by
Esmée, who is too frightened to admit strangers during Jack's
absence. On his return from a neighboring mine, Jack learns from
Esmée of the visitor, but it is too late. He finds his brother's
lifeless body on the mountainside and brings it to the cabin for
Esmée to guard, while he seeks others to help him bear the
corpse to the community below. During her vigil the conscience-
stricken Esmée reviews the fateful events that have transpired,
concluding that the innocent victim before her symbolizes the
family ties she has wronged. Thus when she is warned by a
mountain neighbor of the increasing fury of the storm and the
probability of an avalanche, she refuses to leave the cabin,
welcoming death as a means of punishment and escape.
Ultimately she is entombed, with the body of Jack's brother, by a
torrent of snow.

Marred as the four tales are by strained coincidences and
melodramatic resolutions, they nonetheless comprise a memorable collection. The bleakness of the lava fields and the snow
fields, the hopelessness of the triangular attachments, the
awesomeness of brute nature—these are elements which invest
Foote's volume with what one impressed reviewer termed its
"sad poetic quality."[35] That the tales are irrepressibly romantic,
albeit "darkly" so, is particularly apparent when they are
compared with any volume of realistic fiction published at the
same time—with Sarah Orne Jewett's *The Life of Nancy, and*

Other Tales (1895), for example. Foote's stories are closer in theme to those collected in Bret Harte's *A Protegée of Jack Hamlin's* (1894); in treatment they resemble Frank Norris's naturalistic "romances" in *A Deal in Wheat* (1893). In other words, despite the grimness of the settings, despite the naturalistic forces against which the characters are pitted, the tales convey impression rather than substance, and appeal to emotions rather than intellect.

Like Foote's earlier Idaho tales, these dark romances indulge the desires of their author by providing the necessary escapes, for they are a grim working out of her fears and fantasies. Neither the prototypal eastern man coarsened by life in the West (Ludovic, Henniker, Esmée's husband), nor the sensitive male figure offering the heroine escape (the Swede, Jack Waring), nor even the woman betrayed (Phebe, Callie) emerges unscathed; but Foote is hardest on the heroine as betrayor (Meta, Rose, Esmée). A product of the Victorian era, Foote worshipped propriety in her fiction as in her life. If ever her own course veered from the track, "if ever a cog slipped,"[36] her capacity for pain was far greater than her toleration of shame; equipoise was to be regained, whatever the cost. In her stories death served as a restorative, as an escape; in her life, years of silence served to smooth the anguish of her bleak life in the canyon and of her determined struggle to remain loyal to a man blighted by the West.

Mary Hallock Foote suspected in 1895, while preparing her title story and the rest of the volume for publication, that relief was imminent; for in January of that year James Hague had summoned Arthur to install a pumping plant for the North Star Mining Company, Hague's enterprise in the Sierra mining town of Grass Valley, California. What began there as a provisional assignment became within two years a permanent position, a haven Arthur and Mary had earned after their "twelve years' siege and surrender"[37] in Idaho. The security and stability which had eluded them was at last within reach; by fall the brightened prospects for the future justified transporting the Foote family to Grass Valley. Mary's joyous September reunion with Arthur and the Hagues, reminiscent of her first arrival in California nineteen years before, proved a welcome omen that the "gray and rugged passage" of her life had come to an end.

A.   "Picturesque Aspects of Farm Life in New York,"
Scribner's Monthly

B. *The Skeleton in Armor*

C. "Pictures of the Far West," *Century Magazine*

D. "Pictures of the Far West," *Century Magazine*

E. "The Century Series of American Artists," *Century Magazine*

CHAPTER 5

Repose

THE first years following Mary Hallock Foote's move to Grass Valley—located about fifty miles northeast of Sacramento, California—represented a tranquil period marked by personal satisfactions. Between 1896 and 1903 she saw her family prosper in a setting of "perfect peace and health": she described it to Helena as a place of "lovely sights always before one's eyes; quiet sounds; excellent food and fruit & milk and cream. It isn't good for my pseudo-Art, but very good for everything else." Arthur became Superintendent of the North Star Mines, and the venture proved immensely profitable for the next twenty years. Arthur Burling completed his university education and accepted his first engineering assignment—in Korea—while Betty likewise developed talents inherited from her parents: she enrolled in 1901 in the Philadelphia School of Design and published her first poem in 1903. Agnes, the youngest, lived at North Star Cottage between school terms. At last, it seemed as if each member of the family had found that elusive "angle of repose," which, Mary noted, "one finds and loses from time to time but is always seeking in one way or another."[1]

It was during this period that Mary Hallock Foote unofficially retired from the world of art. With her age advancing and her literary success assured, she found the time propitious for completing the artistic withdrawal she had begun more than sixteen years before. Despite the fact that her work continued to command high prices—as, for example, $470 for ten illustrations to accompany her 1896 story, "The Harshaw Bride"—she accepted very few commissions; the handful of works by other authors which she did consent to illustrate were noteworthy items, such as the projected edition of Kipling's *Naulahka* and a volume of Bret Harte. When to her art editor at Houghton Mifflin she attributed her slowdown to failing skill and changing

fashions, the response was an immediate reaffirmation of her
talent:

I am more than ever impressed with the fact that you have, while
retaining all your skill, never lost its youthful freshness. You are
therefore quite mistaken in supposing that any one, least of all our firm,
considers your work old-fashioned. . . . As long as you are willing to
make pictures we are unwilling that any illustrated Edition of our
leading authors' works should be issued without something from your
hand.[2]

Though by the end of the century Foote had virtually ceased
all commissioned illustrating, contemporaries who studied her
integrity of execution never lowered their estimates of her
ability. Edwin Austin Abbey is said to have "frankly envied" her
talents: the story is told of his laboring long over a particular
drawing, only to conclude with exasperation, "I'm trying to get
the feeling that Mary Hallock Foote puts into her work—and I
can't." Joseph Pennell, at the end of his own distinguished career,
averred that Foote "was one of our best illustrators."[3] Of the
several tributes published by critics and fellow artists, no
remarks were more perceptive than those which appeared in the
August 1900 issue of *Critic:*

. . . [Mary Hallock Foote] has occupied a field to herself, perhaps
because of the distinct types which interpret her own text, depicting a
remote environment, and her art has thus been preserved from
imitators and has held its own. Removed from the stress of
commercialism through her residence in the West, she has not done so
much work, taking into account the number of years she has been
familiar to the reading public, but she has thereby escaped the rut and
strain of overwork and has kept her perception fresh and spontaneous;
she has made every individual drawing count. . . .
    [Her art] possesses that intrinsic quality that we would least part
with; its intimacy is appealing, and it has strength and vigor. Pastoral,
elemental, with the earth-feeling throbbing through it, but essentially
poetic and spiritual, it is more the psychic expression of force and
delicacy.[4]

I *"How the Pump Stopped at the Morning Watch"*

With economic stability in California, Foote found the
necessity for hasty publication replaced by the opportunity for

reflection; the majority of her subsequent writing mirrors a
newfound sureness of touch and marks a transition from romance
to realism. In addition to collecting her juvenile tales in *The
Little Fig-Tree Stories* in 1899, she wrote and published by 1902
the four stories of *A Touch of Sun* as well as two novels. Yet
during this period, she departed uncharacteristically from the
pattern of using her real-life locale as the setting for her fiction;
only three tales, one from *A Touch of Sun* and two which were
never collected, utilize a Grass Valley setting.[5] One of these
latter ranks with "The Story of the Alcázar" as her finest short
fiction. Entitled "How the Pump Stopped at the Morning
Watch," it was inspired by an actual occurrence, but unlike her
Idaho and Colorado fiction, it alters reality not in order to escape
it but in order to capture its essence. As Wallace Stegner has
noted, Foote's letters recounting the two unrelated incidents
upon which the story is based show that the facts have been
skillfully transmuted "to arrive at a human truth larger than the
factual truth."[6] The epistolary accounts of the two episodes—the
death of the North Star pump-man and the later breakdown of
the pump—are interesting in their own right:

There was a tragedy in the mine the other day. John Thomas, an
Englishman, who had been pump-man at the North Star for many
years, was killed in the shaft. . . . I saw them carrying the old man by
the house, on a mattress, . . . His arms were bare to the elbow and
crossed on his breast, and white in the sun as bleached bones—His head
was wrapped in something red, and his profile was majestic in its
endurance and its pallor—and its *age*. The age of toil. . . . They think
that this man, for some time, has not been quite right in his head. . . .
No one spoke of this, for fear it might lose him his place; and they were
not certain of his symptoms: but now it is thought that he did not know
what he was doing when he came out into the hoisting shaft, and an
empty car struck him going down, and dragged him a hundred
feet. . . . [H]is long years of service in the depths of the mine had
strained his faculties. (October 16, 1896)

We have had a catastrophe at the North Star. The great spur wheel
that drives the pump broke, three days ago, with a sound like the
explosion of a magazine. The pump is old and the iron had crystallized.
The pump rod is one half mile long! descending the incline shaft (Main
Shaft) and driving six or seven pumps at different stations, down to the
2000 foot level. All these pumps are stopped now, and the water is
rising in the lower levels. Arthur is in San Francisco, attending to the
casting of a new wheel. (February 7, 1897)

In her story, Mary Hallock Foote recasts these two events into a compelling rendition of the bewildered pump-man's last days. We learn that John Trenberth is so completely devoted to the subterranean pumps he oversees that he has become almost one with the machinery: "He looked, when he came on top, like some old piece of mining machinery that has been soaking underground for half a century—plastered with the pallid mud of the deepest levels, coated with grease, and stained with rust from fondlings of his pumps, the recognizably human parts of him—his unsunned face and hands—pitted and drawn with steam."[7] In spite of the pleadings of his wife and friends, Trenberth will not reduce the length of time he works nor desist from overtime; rather, he descends into the shaft at unlikely hours, "imprisoned in a tube of darkness between the crashing of the cars on the one hand and the squeeze of the rod on the other" (470). One summer day the old miner loses his bearings, is struck by an empty hoistcar, and is borne home to die. According to the mining captain, "he'd slipped a cog, somehow" and forgotten the dangerous nature of the surroundings below. For three days Trenberth struggles against death, crying out with his last breath that the Morning Watch pump has stopped. At the same moment two miles away, the mine watchman hears the pump wheel break and stop "with its last stroke":

One little cog, worn out, had dropped from its place; then two cogs came together, tooth to tooth, and the ten-ton wheel burst with a groan that had arrested the passing soul of the pump-man, duty bound to the last.

An old mine, or an old man, that is nearly worked out may run for years, at small expense, if no essential part give way; but the cost of heavy repairs is too great a strain upon halting faith and an exhausted treasury. Even so small a thing as the dropping out of one little cog, in a system worth thousands to rebuild, may decide the question whether to give up or keep on. (471)

In "How the Pump Stopped at the Morning Watch," Foote transcends the prosaic by endowing her materials with humanistic and symbolic import. She makes Trenberth's end, and that of the pump he was bound to, a fitting culmination to his life, for the "constitutional affinity" between the pump-man and his pump is the central metaphor of the tale. Just as the pump parts are worn away from years of use, so Trenberth's agility and sense of bearings are slowly worn down until at last pump and man are virtually indistinguishable. And out of the background emerges an antagonist more awesome than either and superior to both: the irresistible, remorseless force of Nature. The "subterranean sobs and gulpings" which beleaguer Trenberth underground triumph at the end as Nature relentlessly claims its long-denied prerogative: "While they were preaching the funeral sermon, his old enemy, the water of the black deeps, was creeping up, regaining ground which he and the pumps had fought for and defended, inch by inch and year by year" (472). With its striking scenes of the dazed pump-man blinking at the unfamiliar sunlight, the forlorn procession bearing him home, and his wife's distress at his last words, the story remains etched in the reader's memory. At the unlikely age of fifty-two, Mary Hallock Foote had composed a tale whose claim to kinship with the best of the local-color tradition is secure.

II A Touch of Sun

In the same month that Foote published "How the Pump Stopped at the Morning Watch," Bret Harte published a landmark essay asserting that the success of the American short story was due to its "treatment of characteristic American life, with absolute knowledge of its peculiarities and sympathy with its methods; with no fastidious ignoring of its habitual expression, . . . with no moral determination except that which may be the legitimate outcome of the story itself; with no more elimination than may be necessary for the artistic conception. . . ."[8] In her earlier writing, Foote had only twice—in the "Alcázar" and "Morning Watch" stories—achieved this desired freedom from contrivance; most of her short fiction, in point of fact, had been avowedly romantic rather than realistic. But between 1895 and 1900 she wrote a series of stories that aspired to realist ideals. Collected under the title *A Touch of Sun and Other Stories* (1903), these four tales, equally divided between Idaho and California settings, mirror the author's newfound sense of ease and uplifted spirits in Grass Valley. In terms of technique, they reflect Foote's transition during this period to the more metaphorical works of her later years, while in theme they also suggest a shift of emphasis: affairs of the heart are viewed not only from the young lovers' perspective but also from that of their parents. The stories depict the delicate relationships between generations and reflect parental concerns that Mary Hallock Foote faced at Grass Valley. Writing to Helena in 1897, the author had noted, "Well, it is middle-age with us. The time for planning and organizing the children's lives—the choosing of schools, which decides the choice of friendships, on which perhaps marriage—the whole future of a fraction of the race—depends! . . . We are our children's destiny, at this period. Later we fall off like the seed-pod, after its work is done."[9] The tales collected in *A Touch of Sun* focus on parents questioning the wisdom of their children's marriage choices, a theme which would attain fuller development in *The Ground-Swell* (1919).

The earliest of the stories in terms of composition is "The Harshaw Bride," whose plot and setting were suggested by the Footes' excursion in 1894 to Thousand Falls, Idaho.[10] Mr. and Mrs. Tom Daly, modeled after Arthur and Mary, are depicted as a mature couple who provide the stable background against which the volatile romance of Kitty Comyn and Cecil Harshaw is staged. As in *The Chosen Valley* and *Coeur d'Alene*, differences of nationality as well as of generation are played off against each other: the Dalys are easterners living in Idaho, Kitty is a British visitor, and Cecil Harshaw and his brother Micky are British émigrés to the West. The story is presented from the point of view of Mrs. Daly, whose correspondence to her sister provides the narrative framework of the story. Like many of Foote's earlier heroines, Kitty Comyn is a beautiful young woman placed at a disadvantage by unexpected circumstances and thereby made vulnerable to courtship by default. After traveling to Idaho on word from her fiancé, Micky Harshaw, she makes a shocking discovery. It is Cecil rather than his brother who has sent the summons of love; Micky, meanwhile, has embarked upon a hasty marriage. Embarrassed by her predicament, the jilted girl is invited by the Dalys to join their expedition to Thousand Springs; she may pay her way by making drawings of the hydraulic machinery that Daly investigates. During the course of the trip Kitty is won over by Cecil, who was also invited; he proves to be a well meaning suitor who has always loved her and who, like Lochinvar, hopes to save his lady from marriage to a lesser rival.

Another of the stories, "The Maid's Progress," is fashioned out of many of the same elements as "The Harshaw Bride" but is slighter and does not include marriage by default.[11] Once again the love interest is an implied triangle, with one participant absent and with a surrogate parent figure looking on. Daphne Lewis, beautiful and artistic like Kitty Comyn, accompanies her uncle Reverend Withers to Idaho to find the precise locale where his son Jack—who had been Daphne's suitor—was fatally assaulted two years before. With the aid of Thane, Jack's friend from Idaho who joins the expedition, Withers plans to transform the murder site into a memorial to his son. But his hopes are shattered when the exact spot cannot be located, and the hollow which the wayfarers determine may be the ill-fated Pilgrim Station fills him with apprehension.

As in Hawthorne's "The Hollow of the Three Hills," the bleakness of the locale works to strip the characters of all pretension. In the desolate setting, Foote's heroine, like Hawthorne's, relives and acknowledges her guilt; she, too, is not what she appears to be. She confesses to her uncle that she has no claim to consolation or to the epithet "maiden widow" he insists upon; she had not reciprocated Jack's love and had never intended to marry him. While Daphne struggles to extricate herself from the bonds of the past, Thane does likewise. He confides to Withers that he and Jack were estranged by a quarrel before the latter's death. Then Thane seeks Withers's permission to sue for the hand of Daphne, whom he has come to love during the course of the journey. Disheartened by these painful disclosures, Withers at last decides, like the Dalys before him, to allow love its course. The wagon party disbands, with Daphne and Thane arranging to reunite some days later in *Bliss*, Idaho.

"Pilgrims to Mecca," a variation on Foote's favorite theme of East versus West, is an ironic piece about the dilemma faced by upper-class parents in the West who want to secure for their children the advantages of an eastern education. In 1891 Foote had considered moving to be near Arthur Burling when he entered the Massachusetts Institute of Technology, but had abandoned the idea. The move would not have been that unusual for the time, for the question of whether a mother and child should sacrifice present happiness for uncertain future benefits—should, in other words, forsake the West for "that old fetich of the East" (148)—was one which many mothers answered affirmatively. What most aroused Foote's literary interest in the predicament was the case of mothers who, instead of questioning, accepted without reservation the necessity of such transcon-

tinental uprooting. As she would record in her *Reminiscences,*
she had observed during her first westbound train journey in
1876 a San Francisco matron and her daughter who, for the sake
of the girl's education, had resided in the East and in Paris for
two years. The daughter, Foote noted, seemed undisguisedly
relieved to be going "home."[12]

A railroad journey provides the framework for "Pilgrims to
Mecca" and offers a clue to its meaning. The Valentins, mother
and daughter, embark very early from San Francisco on a
Boston-bound train; the mother's haste is underscored symbolically by her later admission, "We started wrong" (173).
During the journey she attempts to justify their painful
separation from Mr. Valentin by enumerating the "exceptional
social opportunities" awaiting Elsie. Singling out a fashionably
dressed mother and daughter aboard, Mrs. Valentin assures Elsie
that eastern training is superior and recognizable, as the
demeanor of the pair demonstrates. It is with such admirable
specimens of the eastern girl, Mrs. Valentin continues, that Elsie
will soon be pursuing her education.

Foote's story of the Valentins' journey achieves depth through
the addition of a counterpointing motif—the casualties of war.
Set in the summer of 1898, the tale contrasts the mother's
superficial concerns of correct clothing and behavior with the
seriousness of mounting losses from the Spanish American war.
"The lists from El Caney were throbbing over the wires, and the
country, so long immune from peril and suffering, was awakening
to the cost of victory" (168–69). At each of the train stops, Elsie
peruses the station bulletin boards for war news. Learning from
Elsie that Billy Castant, one of the girl's admirers, has enlisted,
Mr. Valentin begins to understand her daughter's concern; when
Elsie confides that Billy proposed marriage to her, the mother
comes to realize how much the younger generation has already
known of life.

The train reaches Chicago and the Valentins, having made the
mistake of not taking the direct express, must stay overnight;
here "the war pressure seemed to close in upon them" (168). In
their hotel they receive a visit from their bishop, lately
transferred to an eastern diocese, who advises Mrs. Valentin that
Elsie should not be hurried: "Her education will come as God
sends it" (174). He reveals that Elsie's classmates in the
prestigious Boston finishing school, contrary to the Valentins'

expectations, will all be western girls—and will include the young lady on the train whom they earlier assumed to be eastern. As the bishop leaves, he tells Mrs. Valentin that Elsie's education has already begun: news of the charge at San Juan has just arrived, and Billy Castant is listed among the casualties. The Valentins depart Chicago, not for mecca but for home. Awakened to the fact that "with experience, as with death, it is the prematureness that hurts," Mrs. Valentin no longer urges the superficial or the unknown upon her daughter. "It is eye to eye and heart to heart, and only straight talk between them now, as between women who know" (176).

"A Touch of Sun," the best story of the collection, also deals with a young girl prematurely experienced and with "straight talk between women who know," but it is a much more delicately wrought tale. Taking for its setting Grass Valley and North Star Cottage during the dry season, the story quickly establishes the "hotbed climate" which serves as central metaphor:

The trees were young, too quickly grown; like child mothers, they had lost their natural symmetry, overburdened with hasty fruition. . . .
    "How everything rushes to maturity here! The roses blossom and wither the same hour. The peaches burst before they ripen. Don't you think it oppresses one, all this waste fertility, such an excess of life and good living, one season crowding upon another?" (10)

Margaret Thorne, the mining superintendent's wife who poses this question, has returned from the coolness of the mountains to her home in the mining community in order to meet a domestic crisis. The prematurely blossoming landscape, the roses blighted by "a touch of sun," foreshadow Mrs. Thorne's concern: her son Willy has become engaged to a young woman whom she and her husband know to have been compromised in the past. Mrs. Thorne hesitates between incurring her son's displeasure by disclosing the story of Helen Benedet's youthful indiscretion, or jeopardizing his future happiness by remaining silent. After consulting her husband she determines to write, unaware that Helen is on the way to meet them and to confess her past.

Like the blighted heroine of Browning's *A Blot in the Scutcheon* and the flawed Charlotte Stant of James's soon-to-be-published novel *The Golden Bowl*, Helen Benedet is a beautiful young heiress who has become engaged without confessing to her questionable relations with an earlier suitor. Seven years before, sequestered as a "jeune fille" on her family's ranch, she had grown restive under the strains of heat and enforced isolation. Having tasted little freedom, the sixteen-year-old acquiesced one evening to an all-night ride with a handsome stable hand:

> . . . [H]e took command, not roughly or familiarly, but he no longer used the third person, as I had instructed him, in speaking to me. The first time he said "you" it sent the blood to my face. We were far up the mountain then, and morning was upon us.
>
> I wish to be definite here. From the moment I saw him plainly face to face the illusion was gone. Before, I had seen him by every light but daylight, and generally in profile. The profile is not the man. It is the plan in outline, but the eyes, the mouth, tell what he has made of himself. So attitude is not speech. As a shape in the moonlight he had been eloquent, but once at my side, talking with me naturally—I need not go on! From that moment our journey was to me a dream of horror, a series of frantic plans for escape. (56)

On the Oakland ferry she had appealed for aid to a nameless passenger who arranged her escape and her return—tarnished but virginal—to family. The passenger was Mr. Thorne, who, with his wife, kept the girl's secret, never dreaming their son would one day meet and fall in love with her. Helen, too, is surprised and unprepared for the recognition scene at the Thornes'; and after recounting to them the details of her onetime indiscretion, she strengthens her resolve to free their unsuspecting son by breaking the engagement. But Willy, on receiving his mother's letter, journeys home to explain that he has known of Helen's past all along.

Foote prepares the reader for the fact of Willy's prior knowledge by drawing an explicit parallel with *A Blot in the Scutcheon*. When Willy, describing Helen by letter, maintains that she is "a woman like a dew drop" (13), Mrs. Thorne recognizes the quotation from Browning's drama and wonders whether her son knows its context. The answer turns out to be yes. Like Lord Tresham reflecting on his sister Mildred, Mrs. Thorne thinks Helen brazen to engage herself to one man when she has been compromised earlier by another; but as in the case of Tresham, Mrs. Thorne is unaware that Willy, like Mildred's Merton, knows his fiancée's past and considers her "purer than the purest."[13] Foote's tale does not conclude melodramatically with the death of the three principals, as in the Browning version; rather, the story's strength lies in its quiet, restrained conclusion. Willy's arrival during Helen's visit implies a renewal of vows. Though Mrs. Thorne greets him with the warning, "Don't, for pity's sake, be hopeful!", Willy—who "saw most things that he looked at, and when he aimed for a thing he usually got somewhere near the mark" (79)—strides determinedly across the sun-baked landscape to proclaim his love.

The striking pictorial effects of "A Touch of Sun," coupled with its unusual situation and realistic characters, make the story linger in the reader's memory long after the companion pieces are forgotten. Yet all the stories in the collection possess a charm of style and arrangement not present in earlier tales. As a reviewer observed, "In two or three sentences Mrs. Foote can touch up the interior of a Pullman car with its occupants, or stand a woman in the open door of a shack in the prairie, or scoop out a hollow in a plateau so vividly that the reader sees the object described unforgettably."[14] The tales are a tribute to Foote's corner of the world—to the heat and roses of California, and the dust and desolation of Idaho. As such, they represent further evidence of her commitment to the western scene and confirm her as one of the period's leading interpreters of the West. Charles Lummis, surveying western literature around the turn of the century, observed that all of Foote's recent work was characterized by "that undefinable but unmistakable largeness of soul which belongs to our horizons" and declared:

If those who have carefully followed American literature for the last ten years were bidden to make choice of the most typical series of Western stories written by a woman, I fancy a majority would promptly elect Mary Hallock Foote. Western in very truth of scene and "color" and outlook, marked by all the instincts at once of woman, artist, poet, and story-teller, *The Led-Horse Claim* and its fellows are of a quality that refuses to be forgotten.[15]

A Touch of Sun proved to be Foote's last volume of tales; though she wrote a handful of stories in the succeeding years, they remained uncollected. Freed from illustrating deadlines and the pressures of transcontinental migration, Mary Hallock Foote directed her energies toward full-length fiction. As the century turned a corner, so did her writing career: between 1900 and 1919 Foote published seven successive novels, the last two of which—written as she entered her seventies—rank among the very best of her fictional canon.

III   The Prodigal

Foote spent the five winter months of 1898–99 living, as she explained to Helena, in San Francisco in "one of the houses that came around the Horn in sections and was put together out here." In February, when *McTeague*—Frank Norris's electrifying story of San Francisco—appeared, she was deeply engrossed writing her own novel of the city. Upon its publication seventeen months later, one critic was so enthusiastic as to exclaim, "No one, I think, has ever written a more compelling story of San Francisco."[16] While few modern readers would rank *The Prodigal* over *McTeague,* which it resembles only in painstaking fidelity to locale, the work provides ample support for Norris's contention that San Francisco represents one of the best "story cities" in the United States. The opening sentences of *The Prodigal* deftly establish the waterfront setting which dominates the story:

An August fog was drifting inland from the bay, in thin places the blue Contra Costa hills showed through, and the general grayness was tinged with pearl. San Francisco dripped and steamed along her bristling waterfront; derricks loomed black, and yards and topmasts reddened, as a fringe of winter woodland colors up at the turn of the year.[17]

Against the backdrop of bustling docks where the South Seas trade flourishes, Foote develops a tale of two men of British descent—Clunie Robert, a New Zealander, and Morton Day, a New Englander. It is Robert's plight that brings the two together and provides the highly picturesque situations of the story. Consigned to a south sea whaler by his exasperated father, Robert—a "prodigal son"—was shipwrecked off Cape St. Lucas, saved by natives who expected him to marry one of their girls, and sold into servitude aboard a California-bound vessel after he refused. The story opens with his arrival in San Francisco, where he applies for money through the shipping firm with which his wealthy father does business. Though Day, one of the em-

ployees, is instructed to help Robert in small ways, the firm is
authorized to advance Robert only 50 cents a day.

Until his own savings are exhausted, Robert leads a "skyrocket
life of pleasure, founded on the fancy of an idle man" (29), but
once reduced to penury he regains his self-respect. With Day's
help he secures a position as harbor boatman. In this capacity he
becomes involved in the two delicate situations which establish
his character. The first involves the tramp steamer *Sumbawa*,
which is quarantined offshore because of smallpox. When the
ship's captain entreats Robert to smuggle his pregnant wife off
the ship, the New Zealander is torn between obeying the letter
of the law or acknowledging a higher duty. Under extremely
difficult conditions, he rows the woman some forty miles up the
coast, but the strain of the journey takes its toll on them both.
The woman gives premature birth to a son, Robert collapses in
exhausted stupor after fortifying himself with drink, and the
mother dies hours later for want of medical attention. When
Anne Dunstan, sister of the deceased, arrives in San Francisco to
care for the newborn child, a chastened and sober Robert
becomes her right-hand man and, in the process, falls in love
with her.

As the months pass Day notes with approbation Robert's
sobriety and resolve, and is able to offer his friend a minor
position with the shipping firm. Yet one final test of character
awaits. While processing the *Parthenia,* a steamer bound for
Liverpool, Robert discovers that it is dangerously overloaded
and that one of its passengers is Concha, the girl from St. Lucas
whose favor he courted and then spurned. Learning also that she
is now the mother of a light-skinned son, he assumes the child to
be his and feels a moral obligation to save the pair or to share
disaster with them. He goes aboard the *Parthenia* on the day of
its departure to face his fate, and his selflessness is rewarded:
Concha surprises him by revealing that she is married to a
seaman presently stationed in England and by agreeing to
disembark from the ship. The *Parthenia* sinks as it goes out the
Golden Gate, but Robert's fortunes rise: within weeks Anne
accepts his proposal of marriage and his family summons him
home. The errant son has been tested by his experiences and not
found wanting; he returns East, a better man for having been
West.

Concerned that her story might not meet the standards of

literary decency, Mary Hallock Foote sought the opinions of
Richard and Helena Gilder. They assured her that despite the
hero's implicit sexual liaison with Concha and his excessive
drinking, the novel was eminently publishable; but Foote
continued to have misgivings even after the work appeared in
print:

. . . [I]t is not a woman's story. *How* I wish I had a son who would put
his name to my stories. One could write so much better if one were not
a woman—a wife and mother of young girls—the fields beyond where
only men may tread. I know as much about the men who tread those
fields as a man could—more—but I don't know the fields and don't wish
to appear to.[18]

Such concerns may seem groundless today, but for Mary Hallock
Foote, accustomed to the standards of the genteel tradition, they
were real indeed. She was both relieved and gratified when
critics complimented the novel's "strength," "repression," and
"fineness of touch."[19]

As one reviewer noted, Foote's tale suggests comparison with
the fiction of Robert Louis Stevenson—particularly with his
novel *The Wrecker*, published in 1892.[20] It is not unlikely that
Foote may have been influenced by this work, for during the
1880s and 1890s Stevenson's novels were lionized by the reading
public. For an incurable romantic like Mary Hallock Foote, the
British arch-romancer had special charm; his published correspondence as well as four of his novels were shelved within reach
of her writing desk. Though *The Wrecker*, like *The Prodigal*,
concerns the shipping trade and focuses on the relationship
between a young, wealthy English profligate and his American
friend from San Francisco, it is a far more complex tale. It
depends for its chief interest upon an additional character,
whose far-flung business ventures occasion the picturesque
settings of the novel—San Francisco, the South Seas, Australia,
France, and England. In technique, also, the differences between
the two novels are marked: whereas *The Wrecker* is presented as
an involved mystery, *The Prodigal* is designed, like *The Last
Assembly Ball*, as a tripartite drama. If Foote read *The Wrecker*,
its atmosphere and suspense were the elements she most likely
recalled as she began her own novel.

On the other hand, that Foote drew upon the parable of the

Prodigal Son for the framework of her story is beyond doubt. Like his biblical prototype, Robert journeys from his homeland to a foreign country, where he engages in riotous living, suffers deprivations, is convinced of his own unworthiness, and is at last reinstated in his father's good graces. But Foote stresses an essential departure in her tale by quoting, at one point, from Luke 15: "For there was no longer any reasonable, comforting explanation of his father's silence. There was no relenting, to the effect of, 'This my son was dead, and is alive again; he was lost, and is found' " (30). Robert is not immediately accepted by his father once communication between the two is reestablished; for the latter-day prodigal, the path to reacceptance is longer and more arduous. Like Alan Dunsmuir of *The Chosen Valley*, Clunie Robert is tested by an indifferent frontier while his father observes from afar. But unlike young Dunsmuir, Robert finds salvation in the West: once regenerated by his western sojourn, he is confident of paternal acceptance. By the end of the tale he is seeking moral approval rather than financial support, and this change of goals reflects his maturation.

This reversal of pattern in *The Prodigal*, whereby the hero is saved by the West rather than destroyed by it, is evidence of Foote's growing acceptance of the West on its own terms. Given the comfort and security of Grass Valley and the recent indications that Arthur's drinking was under control, Mary Hallock Foote was prepared to grant the West its due. Whereas Harry Conrath *(The Led-Horse Claim)* and Mr. Bingham *(Coeur d'Alene)* had been ruined in the West by drink, and Frank Embury *(The Last Assembly Ball)* had been vanquished because of his eastern past, Clunie Robert triumphs over the ghost of his past (Concha) and the temptations of the West. By recognizing his ordeal as an opportunity, he converts his western experience into capital—thus following the lead of his author, Mary Hallock Foote.

IV   The Desert and the Sown

Because of its effective, realistic characterization, *The Prodigal* surpasses much of Foote's earlier writing, but when compared with the work that follows it, its contrived nature becomes apparent. *The Desert and the Sown*, published in 1902, is a more plausible and more impressive treatment of the sensitive relations between a son and his parents; it is a tragic parable which demonstrates the fundamental nature of certain "carelessly accepted" truths. Drawing upon the same biblical story which inspired *The Prodigal*, Foote achieves in *The Desert and the Sown* an intensity absent in the previous novel.

The Desert and the Sown is Mary Hallock Foote's first work written wholly in the realist vein. It grew out of a low-keyed story which Richard Watson Gilder had related to her, a true tale she amplified and improved upon. To reinforce its verisimilitude she chose the settings with which she was most familiar—the wilderness of Idaho and the farmland of New York—and depicted the psychology of those whom she knew best: the husband who, after long years of professional exile, has become humbled and blunted by the West, and the wife who, uncomfortable in the West, desires haven in the East yet knows it to be haunted by the past. The effect of Foote's transmutations confirms her authorial comment that "reality has its own convincing charm, not inconsistent with plainness or even with commonness. To know it is to lose one's taste for toys of the imagination."[21] Choosing as title a line from the *Rubáiyát* of Omar Khayyam, Foote composed her tale slowly, likening it to a patchwork quilt done "a bit at a time." In December 1901, when it had become her first novel ever rejected for serial publication, she expressed her confidence in it, writing to Helena, "I shall never do anything better or duller. . . . Yet it is good too. I'll be hanged if it isn't. But it isn't the popular thing, and any good editor would say so."[22]

Foote was referring to the criticism of Bliss Perry, assistant editor of the *Atlantic,* to whom she had submitted the manuscript. Perry's appraisal was favorable, so favorable that he engineered for the novel a more remunerative contract with Houghton Mifflin than Foote had ever had before, yet he recognized the story's serious limitations as a serial. He noted that it tended "to avoid the dramatic climaxes which are naturally expected by the reader," that its "psychological thread would be seriously broken by the necessary interruption of monthly installments," and that the plot was "more or less unpleasant, even antipathetic to the mood of the ordinary magazine reader." Foote, he commented, had to be prepared in writing a realistic novel to accept the risk of "alienating the sympathy of some readers."[23] When *The Desert and the Sown* appeared as a book in the spring of 1902, the reviews were primarily favorable, with several critics hailing the work as a tragedy in which the characters were stripped of their social pretensions and forced to expose their spiritual selves. But the reviewers did not pose the crucial question of *whose* tragedy the story treats. Foote's novel is a complex interweaving of four lives, a tale of husband, wife, son, and daughter-in-law in which the positions of the principal characters shift according to the pressures exerted against them. In this fiction, as in life, it is frequently difficult to distinguish the protagonist from the antagonist.

Although the plot covers only the three years between the wife's arrival in Idaho and her husband's death in New York, the story spans the family's fortunes for two generations, underscoring the weight of the past on the present. At the center is the love affair of Emily and Adam, she the daughter of wealthy Abraham Van Elten and he a hired man on her father's New York farm. Despite Van Elten's threats to disinherit her, Emily elopes with Adam to the West where, in time, Adam becomes a teamster, Emily a mother, and both are reduced to a hand-to-mouth existence. During one of their frequent moves the couple are unexpectedly separated, with the pregnant Emily and her son Paul staying in the stationkeeper's house to await Adam's return. After three days she can endure the suggestive leers of the keeper no longer and with relief accepts a ride from one of her husband's friends passing through on his way East. Though she leaves a letter of explanation for Adam with the stationkeeper, she never again hears from her husband and fears him dead. Eventually her father offers to reinstate her if she will renounce Adam's name; instead, Emily repudiates her father, who then retreats to his tower bedroom "in the old rat-ridden house up the Hudson" (57). Abraham dies intestate, "his negative way of owning his debt to nature at the last" (57), making it possible for the "widow" Bogardus and her two children to lead a life without want.

Through the years Emily remains unaware that Adam returned to One Man Station the night she left. When the keeper enraged Adam with his leering taunts and lies, Adam struck and killed him. Filled with fear and shame, Adam determined that the only way to spare his wife this new humiliation was to disappear. For twenty years he wandered the West in penance for his crime, living the solitary life of a packer and assuming the name of "John Hagar." It is through their son that Emily and Adam are unexpectedly reunited. Betrothed to Moya Middleton, Paul invites his mother to Idaho for the wedding preparations and then departs on a hunting trip to which he has long been pledged. Packer John Hagar leads the hunting group, which becomes trapped in a life and death situation; during the crisis comes mutual recognition, with John and Paul each learning for the first time the "other" side of the story. Once the two are rescued, father convinces son that Emily Bogardus must be given the option of choosing *not* to accept her husband, for he knows his fortunes have declined while hers have improved over twenty years. When the unsuspecting woman is ushered alone into Adam's presence and his secret is revealed, her dismay and hesitation deeply wound him. He withdraws all claims, spares her his side of the story, and bolts into the comforting Idaho wilderness.

The last half of the tale is concerned with Paul's attempts to find his father and to understand his mother's private repudiation of her husband. While he and Moya slowly track Adam during their protracted wedding journey eastward, they are unaware that the shock of rejection has broken him in mind and left but one desire—to die at "home" on the Van Elten farm. Mrs. Bogardus, also unaware of Adam's state or whereabouts, busies herself in New York preparing the Van Elten estate for the arrival of her son and daaghter-in-law. There she finds herself painfully confronting the past again and again—in cleaning the bedroom of the man whom she would not acknowledge as her father, in passing through the fields where labored the man whom she will not acknowledge as her husband, and in bracing to meet the son who condemns her "unimpeachable widowhood." Thus on old Abraham's estate the final drama is played out: for years the lives of Adam, Emily, and Paul "have been shaping towards this meeting" (131).

In the poignant but forced ending, the decrepit Adam makes his way unnoticed to Abraham's old room; it is only when he is discovered, starving and delirious, by his infant grandson John that the final reckoning occurs. A shocked and saddened Emily wishes to acknowledge publicly the dying man as her husband, but her son intervenes. Long before dawn on the day of Adam's funeral, Paul goes to his mother, forgiving her and repenting his own false pride. He recognizes at last that the man who was Adam Bogardus died at One Man Station, and he asks that the dead be allowed to rest in peace:

"Every hand he loved was against him—bruising his gentle will. Each one of us has cast a stone upon his grave. But you took the brunt of it. You spoke out plain the denial that was in my coward's heart from the first. And I judged you! I—who uncovered my father's soul to ease my own conscience, and put him to shame and torture, and you to a trial worse than death. . . .

"All that came after . . . his last solemn recantation does not touch the true spirit of his sacrifice. It was finished. My father died to us then as he meant to die. The body remained—to serve out its time, as he said. . . . This is how he loved us!" (311–12)

As the long night's journey into day draws to a close, a chastened son and mother are ultimately reunited by Adam's sacrifice and redeemed by his love.

The final passage of the novel reinforces the Christian framework which Foote deftly uses throughout. The expulsion of Adam and Emily from the Van Elten pastures, the lonely death of the patriarchal Abraham, the primal curse upon Adam which transforms him into the outcast Hagar, and the humanistic beliefs of Paul which lead to the recognition and conversion in the wilderness—all are suggestive of biblical archetypes. *The Desert and the Sown* depicts the sins of the fathers weighing upon the next generation. Abraham's steadfast refusal to forgive Emily and Adam culminates in his lonely death, while Emily's refusal to acknowledge Adam leads to the latter's wretched demise. It is only in the later generations that the sins of the past are atoned and forgiven: Paul's acceptance of Adam and young John's recognition of his grandfather work through the curse. Peace is restored, and the family "boggard"—the local goblin supposed to haunt a scene of gloom or violence—at last disappears.

The novel is, to a great extent, a testimonial to the insight of Paul and Moya which paves the way to familial reconciliation. The son inherits his father's "gentleness and purity of purpose" (309), and he recognizes the intrinsic worth of Adam, the common man. Whereas Emily was early driven to despair by Adam's plodding nature, Paul revels in the man's native wisdom and homespun philosophy. To Paul, Adam—alias Packer John—is a romantic figure; Paul's references to "Woodnotes" confirm his

perceptions of Adam as the Emersonian "forest seer." After Paul
confides to Moya the story of Adam Bogardus/Packer John, she
also becomes committed to the task of reconciling past and
present: "Nor could she now imagine for themselves any lover's
paradise inseparable from this moral tragedy, which she saw
would be fibre of their fibre, life of their life" (185). Through the
all-accepting, nonaccusing stance of Moya, daughter of the
middle class, the gulf between the "common man" sympathies of
Paul and Adam, and the upper-class attitudes of Emily and
Abraham, is bridged.

With its emphasis on the actions and psychology of the
younger generation represented by Paul and Moya, *The Desert
and the Sown* departs radically from the two nineteenth-century
works which Foote seems to have recalled while writing her tale.
One, Stevenson's *Olalla* (1885), contains several parallel elements: the marriage of a woman of high station to a muleteer, his
disappearance under unusual circumstances, the mother's seclu-
sion with her children in the ancestral home, the mysterious
tower bedroom, always locked. But the family secret being
guarded in Olalla, Spain, is far more grisly than that of Foote's
New Yorkers, and Stevenson's romance ends with the implicit
disintegration of the family. The second work, Victor Hugo's *Les
Misérables*, is alluded to in *The Desert and the Sown*. When one
of Emily's neighbors comments that she may be sheltering a
tramp—a "Jean Valjeans" or "angel unawares"—she becomes
uneasy; though ignorant of the nature of Hugo's hero, Emily
fears the possible identity of a man using her home as a refuge.
Though Packer John has not led as varied a life as Jean Valjeans,
there are similarities between the two. Both have committed a
crime and stand condemned by society, though their actions
were justifiable; both assume a new identity and endure a life of
fear and anguish, and both, as they are dying, are reunited with
their families.

While the Stevenson and Hugo novels furnished some
inspiration, there is little doubt that while writing *The Desert
and the Sown* Foote had foremost in mind the parable of the
Prodigal Son. Just as Clunie Robert "was lost and is found; was
dead and is alive," so Adam and Paul are, metaphorically,
prodigal sons. Adam is lost to Abraham and to Emily and is
resurrected by Paul, while it is only after Emily freely
acknowledges Adam that Paul is restored to *her*. The novel is, in

the final analysis, chiefly Paul's story: it is he who is lost on the hunting expedition and hovers near death, who lives again with his new discovery, who is separated from his mother when she refuses to accept this discovery, and who, at the end of their long night's ordeal, causes his mother to exclaim, "Have I my son—after all?" (313).

This final scene derives its intensity not only from keen characterization but also from the symbolism inherent in the story. "Ten Stone Meadow," the Van Elten pasture where Adam toiled until his arms ached, was "poor man's country." It was not, as one might assume from the novel's title, sown farmland; it was, rather, a land of "stony hillsides, stony roads lined with stone fences. The chief crop of the country is ice and stone" (68). For Adam, but not for Emily, the western wilderness proved more fertile. The meaning of the novel, however, probably inheres less in the ironic contrast between Idaho and New York, or between Adam and Emily, than in the unexpected differences between mother and son. Emily, the rich widow "who had never been at heart a wife," has led a barren life, but Paul, son of the hireling Bogardus, has flourished under the fertilizing influence of the frontier. While the mother was raised in a world dominated by the locked tower bedroom, the son has absorbed the wholesome influence of outdoors and the prized knowledge of the common man. Yet all of Paul's philanthropic sentiment does not sensitize him to the needs of his own mother; only at last, when he actually sees the vast difference between Emily and Adam and recognizes his own nature as partaking of both, is he able to return his mother's love. On this note of reconciliation between past and present Foote closes the novel perhaps best representative of her talent.

V *Personal Tragedy*

With the favorable reception of *The Desert and the Sown* in 1902 and *The Cup of Trembling* in 1903, Mary Hallock Foote was in excellent spirits as she began her most ambitious literary project to date—an historical novel entitled *The Royal Americans.* But her writing ended when tragedy struck, and the novel begun so eagerly was not completed for six years. As her autobiography indicates, life was never the same after that "ambush of fate" in May 1904.

It was to have been a particularly happy month for Mary and
Arthur: Arthur Burling was returning from his three-year
engineering stint in Korea; Betty was arriving from the East, and
Agnes was coming back from schooling in San Francisco. The
homecoming, however, was never celebrated. Seventeen-year-
old Agnes, earliest to return, was suddenly taken by acute
appendicitis and died at home following emergency surgery.
Three days after the funeral, the stunned mother made her first
painful communications with the outside world. In a poignant
letter to Helena, she recounted the swift finality of the tragedy:

My dearest friend—
     If I could have written to you in the first of this it would have been
easier but there was no time. It was all so quick. This is all there is to
tell—that is, all the Doctors can or will tell us.
     . . . .
     The Doctors left us about sunrise. It was over at 4 in the hot
afternoon. Her poor father had seen her last as she lay on the table
awaiting her ordeal. Then she had said "Dear Daddy" and kissed her
finger to him as he looked back at her. He could not bear the last part—
but just at the last he came and saw the beautiful white dream of peace
on her face. She was unconscious long, long before the end.
     Some mysterious "shock" the Doctors called it—following the
operation. One of the rare cases—not to be accounted for—not a
mental shock for she was not afraid—a shock to the system, fastening
upon the weakest organ: with her the liver, weakened by repeated
malarial fevers.
     In the end it went to her brain.
     She was buried on Saturday—she died on Thursday, May 13—The
miners lined the road for a quarter of a mile on her way—and as they
brought her down to the gate under the cherry trees—the men sang
"Welcome! Welcome!" one of their carols she loved—and the one they
sang at Central Shaft last Christmas when we were there—so happy!
     The hymn we chose for the one to close the service was the "Pax
Tecum" that was sung at Tyringham that dear Sunday with you—when
Agnes held the book with me, and her hand held mine, and she
squeezed hard at the words:
     "Peace, perfect peace, and loved ones far away—" for that morning
we had talked of a second winter in Boston and she had meekly owned
it was best and consented to go through with it. Oh, I am so glad we sent
her nowhere that winter, but kept her home with us.
     Now the experiments in "Education" are over. Our education will
begin now.
     There is not so much to regret. It is more a passion of love, fearing it

did not express itself fully enough while yet there was time.

> Yours lovingly,
> Molly[24]

As a family member recounted long afterward, the death of Agnes was "a blow" from which Foote "never really recovered."[25] Twenty years later, when the author was composing her autobiography, she did not write of the "education" she had received after 1904. Clearly, however, she had summoned forth after the tragedy the self-discipline necessary to ward off emotional collapse. She participated in moving from North Star Cottage, the scene of such recent pain, into the more commodious North Star House that fall, and she continued to serve as director of the Children's Hospital of San Francisco.[26] As the years passed she referred to her bereavement less frequently in letters, but her daughter's image remained present to her throughout. In her valedictory novel *The Ground-Swell*, published in 1919, she recaptured Agnes's essence in the figure of Catherine, and the work is a moving tribute to one girl's beautiful spirit.

Between 1904 and 1910 Foote was disinclined to publish, seeking consolation from and dedicating her energies wholly to the realm of family affairs. From time to time she was asked for interviews, for literary contributions, but her reluctance generally prevailed. To a publisher's request in 1905 for biographical information, she responded that there was little to tell, but the information she did furnish reflects the extent to which she was preoccupied with thoughts of family:

> My work both as an artist and writer has been subordinated constantly, and I may say as a matter of principle, to my home life and its demands. With, to me it seems, the happy result that I have been free from the pangs of competition and the urgency of that need of "success" which makes literature or art such a feverish business for women. I hope this does not sound "preachy."
>
> But after all, it seems to me, as I look back, that this is the thing about my work I am most content with: that I never have allowed it to usurp the chief place.[27]

The one exception to Foote's self-imposed literary silence during this period came when she was asked to contribute to the Spinners' Club benefit fund. The club, composed of San

126 MARY HALLOCK FOOTE

Francisco literati, had decided to publish a collection of short fiction and to assign the proceeds to Ina Coolbrith, the noted California poet. Agreeing to participate, Mary Hallock Foote, along with Gertrude Atherton, Jack London, Frank Norris, Charles Warren Stoddard, and others, wrote a story for the occasion. Published in 1907 and never reprinted, "Gideon's Knock" represents the transmutation of her recent sorrow into a piece of haunting fiction. The setting of the tale, the manager's house at the Consolidated Resumption Mine, is patterned after North Star House, and its first occupants—Mr. and Mrs. Fleming, whose son is in the Far East and whose daughter is in San Francisco—resemble Arthur and Mary Foote. But the tale's unusual narrative framework redeems it from potential sentimentality. A story about the Flemings is related to their successor, Mr. Othet, by the mine's cashier, Joshua Dean. In Conradian style the account which reaches the reader has been filtered through the impressions of listener as well as storyteller, for Othet establishes the occasion and comments upon it.

The story of "Gideon's Knock" is recounted on a stormy evening as the new resident manager and the cashier await the arrival of the eastern mail. Remarking that the man who delivers the mail never knocks at the front door, Othet notes Joshua's uneasiness and presses for the reason. What he learns explains to Othet the "melancholy spell" that pervades the house. According to Joshua, the Flemings' beautiful daughter Constance, when not yet out of her teens, had unexpectedly walked into "an ambush of fate" at home one summer vacation. She had met a visiting foreigner and fell in love, while her stunned parents looked on helplessly:

"They had to let it go on; and he took her away from them six months after she saw him first. That's happiness, if you call it so!"
Again I added, "It is life."
"There was not much left of it in this house after she went," Joshua mused. "It was then they asked me to come up and stay with them. A silence of three does not press quite so close as a silence of two. And we talked sometimes. The mine had taken a great jump; it was almost a mockery the way things boomed."[28]

After marriage Constance moved with her husband to Colfax and communication with her parents became infrequent.

Joshua explains that one stormy winter night when Mrs. Fleming was expecting a letter from Constance, a knock was heard at the door but that Gideon, the faithful watchman and mail deliverer, did not appear. The unexplained knocking continued, at intervals, until Fleming and Joshua called the telegraph office to ascertain the watchman's whereabouts. Learning that Gideon had departed for the Flemings' house a half hour earlier with mail and an urgent telegram, the two men retraced Gideon's path in the snow. At last they discovered his cart, his lantern, and the overturned mail pouch he had recovered at the cost of a fatal misstep down an abandoned mine shaft:

"And the telegram?" I asked.
"It was safe. He'd saved everything, except himself. They were driven over [to Colfax] that night, with not a moment to spare—"
. . . .
"And they were in time?"
"To bid her [Constance] good-by," said Joshua.
"There was no hope for her but in death. Of course, they never explained. She simply fled from—we don't know what. As long as she could she bore it without complaint, and then she came home. . . . It was the only solution left. . . . The logic of her choice was death."
(89-90)

Working through the powerful emotions evoked by the mystery of Agnes's death, Foote makes no attempt in her tale to explain the inexplicable. Neither the phenomenon of the unaccompanied knocking, nor the contents of the telegram, nor the cause of Constance's death is spelled out; rather, Othet—and the reader—are left to draw their own conclusions. The only additional information Othet learns from Joshua is that the Flemings lived in their house but a while longer, moving when they could endure the memories no more, and that the new watchman was instructed to avoid using the door knocker—that baleful reminder of the night Gideon's spirit remained on duty.

The atmosphere of brooding quietness which the tale evokes derives as much from the characterization of Joshua as from the events he relates. During the course of their evening talk Othet comes to suspect that the cashier's loyalty to the Flemings may be alloyed by a considerable personal attachment to the memory of Constance. When, at length, he suggests that Joshua may have stayed on in the manager's house too long, it is Joshua's response which concludes the tale—and which reminds the reader that Foote's story is as much about the pain and mystery of life, as about death:

> "If I have lived here too long for any other reason," he answered gently, "enough has been said. . . . But, as to my mind—I prefer to keep it unhealthy, if by that you mean the tendency to project it a little farther than reason, founded on such laws of the universe as we know, can help us. Healthy minds are such as accept things—endeavor to forget what gives immeasurable pain. *I prefer the pain.*" (90-91; italics mine)

An opaque, haunting story unlike anything else she ever wrote, "Gideon's Knock" offers ample evidence that Foote's skill remained undiminished by her personal tragedy; yet until the anguish relented, she preferred not to write.

VI   The Royal Americans

Sometime late in the decade Mary Hallock Foote resumed and completed the novel she had begun before Agnes's death. She had written to Richard Watson Gilder as early as 1904 that she was in the midst of a sprawling "historical novel" and had—in August 1909—submitted the work to him. For the first time in their thirty-year publishing relationship, however, he was forced to decline one of her manuscripts for the *Century;* its forty-three chapters and numerous major characters made it unsuited for serialization. Gilder's rejection letter, Foote later remarked, "was one of those easy bits of perfection that he could achieve. He didn't want it but he could say so in a way that made you love him. . . . It takes one with a royal nature to tell truth so that you kiss the rod."[29]

Greatly overshadowing the disappointment of rejection was Foote's sorrow soon after on learning of Gilder's death. His passing in November 1909 left a void in her life, for he had been her confidant and mentor since their New York City days so many decades before. Though she declined the invitation to publish a formal eulogy, believing that to be the province of Gilder's more distinguished friends, Foote extolled Richard's

warmth and wisdom to Helena in private letters like the
following:

I think nothing showed his poetic quality more than his gift of
constructive criticism. I don't know how he did it! He certainly did not
mince matters; but he had more turns of phrase, more gay unflinching
ways of lighting on a fault yet not smashing anything that was of any
value. I have chuckled over my own disgrace when he had pointed out
some obvious blemish, and risen up after it in better shape for work
than ever. . . . What droves of us passed through his hands, and I don't
believe he ever gave a pang that was not also a spur. No: he was more
than a critic, more than an editor, more than a good business-man, more
than a poet, more than a perfect friend: he was human, and he was
spiritually human; warm to the best in each of us but never deceived as
to what was the best.[30]

In 1911 Foote was able to write Helena that the manuscript
Gilder had rejected had proved to be "a financial success—as a
book; probably because I followed some of his advice which
wasn't really advice, but a light cast in dark places."[31] Another
factor in the success of *The Royal Americans* was its connection,
albeit belated, with the literary rage which had swept America
at the turn of the century. Historical fiction, costume romance,
"any novel that pretended to a knowledge of the past," was
consumed, as one scholar remarked, "without discrimination, by
the devotees of the form."[32] Among the more meritorious of the
early bestsellers had been S. Weir Mitchell's *Hugh Wynne*
(1897), relating a Quaker's adventures and misadventures during
the American Revolution, Winston Churchill's *Richard Carvel*
(1899), a romance of the Revolution set on both sides of the
Atlantic, and Paul Leicester Ford's *Janice Meredith* (1899), a tale
of the Revolution distinguished for its historical accuracy.
    What *The Royal Americans* shares with these novels, in
addition to period and setting, is a prescribed pattern in which
the hero and heroine, destined for each other from the start, are
at last united despite seemingly insuperable odds, with the
dangers of war lending glamor and requiring heroic sacrifices on
the part of both. While the hero had to be brave and chivalrous,
especially in warfare, the popular appeal of the *fin de siècle*
historical romance derived largely from the qualities of the
heroine. Catherine of *The Royal Americans* is virtually

indistinguishable from Mitchell's Darthea, Churchill's Dorothy, and Ford's Janice Meredith; all conform to an essential outline, as Cecil Williams has explained:

The heroine, a delicate beauty with an appropriate, often exotic, name, is always fortunate—if this be fortunate—in having several lovers to choose from. The reader soon learns which one she will choose, but she doesn't "know her heart" until near the end; . . . She is such a paragon of loveliness that even the finest hero is scarcely worthy of her. . . . There is a fair chance too the heroine will be a refugee, from a corrupt court in Europe, who is now gaining not only the blessings of prospective matrimony but also those of political democracy. . . .[33]

Following the classic pattern, the details of Catherine Yelverton's life comprise the central interest of *The Royal Americans,* for the novel covers the twenty-seven years between Catherine's birth on the eve of Montcalm's victory at Fort Ontario and her marriage at the conclusion of the Revolutionary War.

During the evacuations of Fort Henry and Fort Oswego in 1756, the newborn infant is saved from Indian captivity by the intervention of a French officer; but her aristocratic English mother, weakened from childbirth, dies, and her father, Lieutenant Yelverton of the Royal American forces, is captured. Attended by her nursemaid, Catherine is remanded to the care of Adrian Deyo, a widowed Presbyterian minister related to Yelverton through marriage. In Deyo's home in the Hudson River countryside, she passes a happy childhood, receiving instruction from the minister and playing with Bassy Dunbar, a neighbor boy thought to be of low caste. Catherine's father, restored to the colonial army, monitors her progress from afar. Yelverton arranges that his daughter pay a visit to her prominent godmother, Madame Schuyler of Albany, and that she then go to England to live with her wealthy maternal relatives. He also provides a sister for Catherine: in memory of the man who saved his daughter's life, he adopts a young French girl captured in infancy by Indians and surrendered at the peace treaty of 1763. It is at the Schuyler home that year that Catherine meets her new sister, Charlotte; but she is unprepared for the latter's barbaric manners. Charlotte runs away, Catherine leaves for England, and the two are not reunited for ten years.

Catherine's experiment in British living ends in 1773 when she at last determines that America is her country and that she cannot accept the marriage proposal an aristocratic relative has made her. On a long journey back to the Deyo home, she falls in love with the Quaker Francis Havergal, a fellow passenger and one of her childhood neighbors. For weeks and weeks she postpones rejoining her father at his northern estate in hope that Francis will be able to fulfill his secret pledge and arrange family matters so as to marry. Her old friend Bassy Dunbar, unaware of the secret understanding between Catherine and Francis, silently resolves to ask her hand once the fact of his high-born parentage can be made known. But neither betrothal comes to pass. Heartbroken by irreconcilable religious differences with Francis, Catherine departs for the Yelverton estate some months later.

In the interim, however, Catherine's prolonged absence has triggered a domestic tragedy. Her widowed father, recently successful in recovering the runaway Charlotte, has aroused the gossip of neighboring gentry by inviting his beautiful adopted daughter to live with him. In a belated effort to satisfy the demands of propriety, he convinces Bassy—now recognized as an eminently respectable and wealthy man—to join the household and manage the estate. During the arrangement making, Bassy learns to his chagrin that Catherine is absent because of her secret pledge to marry Havergal. Later, when Bassy hears of the slurs cast upon Yelverton and his innocent ward, he decides to sacrifice his own happiness to save their honor—by marrying Charlotte. Catherine arrives, just after the impromptu wedding, in time only to look on from afar as the mismatched pair begin their loveless wedded life.

As the Revolutionary War breaks upon the Yelvertons and Dunbars, they find themselves torn between conflicting claims: old Colonel Yelverton is a staunch loyalist, Lieutenant Dunbar an avid patriot, and each sister has sworn allegiance to her dearest's cause yet secretly sympathizes with the opposing side. Thus Charlotte and Bassy, in private, are as divided in politics as in their love: though each is devoted to their newborn son, each also views the war as a means of escaping from domestic disappointment. In 1777 the Hudson Valley royalists are routed from their homes and many, like Yelverton, are exiled to Canada. Dispossessed, Catherine, Charlotte, and Charlotte's infant son set forth with the loyalist forces for the haven of Madame

Schuyler's home. But before Albany lies Saratoga, where during the fierce battle Charlotte willingly sacrifices her life; thus it is only Catherine, with Bassy's baby, who is ultimately welcomed by the grande dame. The novel closes just after Burgoyne's surrender, with Captain Bassy Dunbar visiting the Schuyler home and Catherine pledging to marry him when the war concludes. Their union, the author assures us, will be blessed:

They lived to see their heavenly [rain] bow touch earth at the other end, with all the glory of its brightening, its climbing, its fading in rain and mist, between. Bassy brought them home—all three. Catherine rewarded him for the good fight he fought alone, and for his share in the country's battles, and kept him up to his minor duties through a long and honored life.[34]

Like its turn-of-the century predecessors, *The Royal Americans* is an historical romance whose popular appeal stems from the depiction of idealized love and the portrayal of two conflicting sociopolitical forces. In its display of genuine scholarly knowledge and its focus on the heroine's fortunes, Foote's work recalls *Janice Meredith*. But in its emphasis on filial love and sororal conflict, it more closely resembles an early novel by James Fenimore Cooper, her illustrious New York predecessor. While Foote may have had Natty Bumppo in mind when she depicted "Packer John" in *The Desert and the Sown*, she most certainly was thinking in terms of Cooper in her next novel.

Beginning with an allusion to "Deerslayer" on page four, she recreates in *The Royal Americans* certain aspects of the locale and characters Cooper used in *The Spy*. Set in New York's Westchester County in 1750, the latter romance, like Foote's, is a chronicle of family dissension: Frances Wharton, a decidedly American heroine, must prevail over the royalist sympathies of her sister and British father in order to be wooed and won by a Revolutionary patriot. She eventually achieves happiness, while her sister's marital hopes are dashed. But the significance of *The Spy* encompasses more than just domestic conflict; it is a defense of the patriot cause, stressing the role of a man later revealed to be an American double agent. In contrast, Foote's tale has no partisan motivation or additional focus; hers is an effort, and a successful one, at the impartial recording of history. To read *The Spy* is to be caught up with Frances in the cause and the adventure of the American Revolution; to read *The Royal Americans* is to seek with Catherine for repose in a world turned upside down.

Reviewers of *The Royal Americans* justly commented on its excellent workmanship and careful research, for Foote had devoted more time to authenticating the novel's background than even her family realized. Her primary sources were William L. Stone's *The Life and Times of Sir William Johnson* and John Fiske's *Dutch and Quaker Colonies.* Additionally, she borrowed with scrupulous accuracy from the records of General Philip Schuyler, the aristocratic Revolutionary leader who achieved national prominence as a statesman, and from the diary of Baroness de Reidsel, wife of the Brunswick general in charge of the German auxiliary forces. But as in her other novels, Foote also drew upon her own experience. Grounding her story in the locale she knew best, she situated the homes of Adrian Deyo and Bassy Dunbar within her native county, surrounded by the hills and ponds of her own childhood. The Hallock farm is recreated as the Havergal property, and many of the incidents relating to the Havergals—the death of Francis's father, the beautiful composure of the mother, the insufficient legacy, the necessity to retain the mill and millhouse at great cost—had occurred to Mary's own family. *The Royal Americans* is, then, an admixture of personal and national history, romance and imaginative detail. Though lacking the breadth and intensity of *Richard Carvel,* the romantic aura of *Janice Meredith,* or the occasional brilliance of *The Spy,* Foote's work nonetheless deserves comparison with the best examples of its period and genre. In its authenticity of detail, it boasts few rivals.

VII   A Picked Company

The Royal Americans was followed in 1912 by *A Picked Company,* Foote's second, less satisfactory historical romance. Like its predecessor it centers around the competing claims of two "sisters" for the love of one man: the heroine wins, loses, and regains his love; her antagonist, a beautiful foreigner adopted by the family, ultimately loses her life. In the interim the hero is forced to save his father's honor by sacrificing his own happiness and championing the heroine's rival. While *A Picked Company,* a story of the Oregon emigration of the 1840's, thus borrows

elements from *The Royal Americans,* it is neither as panoramic
nor as compelling in presentation. And though like much of
Foote's earlier fiction it focuses on the impact of the frontier
experience upon those who journeyed West, it is marred by
contrivance and by a sterotypic presentation of good and evil.

The tale begins with the disruption of the peaceful life of
Alvin and Silence Hannington, and of their eighteen-year-old
daughter Barbie, by the arrival of Stella Mutrie, Hannington's
orphaned niece from Jamaica whom he has invited to live with
them. Uncomfortable with the rigorous way of life she finds in
Massachusetts, the beautiful outsider flouts convention by
flirting with all the local men, including Jimmy Yardley, Barbie's
favorite beau. When Jimmy's father, the Presbyterian minister of
the community, announces his plans to conduct a party of hand-
picked church members to the Oregon territory, the Hanningtons see the venture as a means of removing Barbie from the
injurious influence of Stella, who has engaged herself not to
Jimmy but to another of Barbie's admirers. The Hannington
family is accepted into the group, as is Jimmy; but on the eve of
the journey Stella too is reluctantly admitted, for, having broken
her engagement, she is once again her uncle's responsibility.
Stella does not confide to anyone that the dashing manner of
Bradburn, the man hired to lead the wagon train, has convinced
her to reject her New England suitor and undertake the journey.

In the summer of 1842 the "picked company" of ten families
begins the overland trek, encountering no major difficulties until
after entering Indian territory beyond Fort Hall, Idaho. At that
point the unity of the group is shattered when the Hanningtons
discover and reveal a private disgrace: the advancing pregnancy
of Stella. Reverend Yardley, serving as leader and lawgiver,
proclaims that both partners in sin must be expelled from the
group; he asks that the man responsible identify himself and
accompany Stella back to Fort Hall. When Bradburn covertly
challenges the minister's authority by refusing to come forward,
Jimmy preserves his father's position, volunteering to undertake
the dangerous escort mission. Before leaving, he reaches a
private understanding with Barbie.

Stella's waywardness, which has brought anguish to both the
Hannington and Yardley families, culminates in tragedy when
Bradburn belatedly acknowledges his responsibility. Overtaking
Stella and Jimmy, he demands that the girl be returned to his

care; but Jimmy, mistakenly believing Stella to have repudiated her lover, refuses. A duel ensues, from which Jimmy emerges victorious. He returns to the wagon train with Stella, who suffered a miscarriage from the long hard ride, and explains his case. The group votes to reaccept him; but for the Yardleys the awful fact of Bradburn's death can never be extenuated, and for the Hanningtons the shame of Stella's pregnancy can never be forgotten.

The last part of the novel briefly recounts the major events befalling the group after its arrival in Oregon's Willamette Valley in 1843. Barbie and Jimmy marry happily, Mrs. Hannington dies, and Reverend Yardley and Mr. Hannington are drawn ever closer together. In contrast, Stella's position in the community remains anomalous; tolerated but not loved, she eventually runs away to San Francisco, where she becomes a celebrated prostitute during the gold rush era. In 1855, desperately seeking to recapture her youth and innocence, she marries a man seven years her junior, but by that time she is hopelessly degenerated in body and spirit. Sickened by a situation from which there is no escape, her husband of less than one year shoots her, then turns the gun on himself.

Foote investigated the historical background of her novel thoroughly, but she incorporates relatively few factual details; figures such as Oregon missionary Marcus Whitman and Hudson Bay Company Superintendent Rae McLoughlin play only cameo roles within the story. Rather, it is the inclusion of incidents from her own life that lends the work its illusion of reality. The poignant details of the Hannington family's uprooting—the solemn packing, the wrenching farewell to an elderly relative whom they knew they would never see again—come from Foote's own first leavetaking for the West in 1876. Certain aspects of the group's overland journey—the lack of privacy, the absence of all conveniences, and the arrival celebration of planting orchards—are other elements of pioneer travel which Foote draws from experience. "When a man sets out an orchard in a new land he plants for his children's children; that soil is his home,"[35] the author explains, adding that in each of the Hannington apple trees "some old parent State sent a little of the sap from her own veins to build up the blood of the Northwest" (407).

The concluding section of *A Picked Company*—a detailed,

explicit account of Stella Mutrie's promiscuity—jars with the
understated manner of the rest of the work, just as the brash
actions of the Jamaican contrast sharply with the civilized
restraint of the New Englanders. The intensity of the final clash
is such that it has a devastating impact on the novel's inner
coherence. The long passages of exposition devoted to Stella's
adventures outside of Oregon are both cumbersome and tedious:
they make what began promisingly as the chronicle of a
circumscribed historical event conclude as an unwieldy exercise
in mediocre fiction. But Foote's frank treatment of Stella, the
only unregenerate female principal in her canon, is significant for
the distance it marks in the author's development. In "The
Trumpeter" eighteen years before, she had depicted Meta, the
adoptee of the Meadows family, as willful and flirtatious; like
Stella, Meta lured away the beau of the "sister" whose room she
shared, faced societal rejection when her pregnancy became
known, and suffered an ignominious death. But whereas Meta's
culpability was diminished and her tragic position enhanced by
her secret marriage and early death, Stella's situation is rendered
uncompromisingly. It is the manner, not the matter, which is
different.

Or again, the difference is the distance between A Picked
Company and The Last Assembly Ball. In 1893, four years after
the publication of her Colorado novel and two years after
Thomas Hardy's Tess of the D'Urbervilles, Foote had asked
Helena concernedly, "We could not produce a 'Tess' in America,
could we?"[36] At that point she did not recognize that her story of
the Colorado frontier, like her later novel of the Oregon trail,
shared basic plot similarities with Hardy's work. All three
recount the misfortunes of a woman who is seduced and
betrayed at an early age, whose later marital happiness is
thwarted because of her past, and whose fatal marriage ends in
the suicide-death of her or her lover. But it is in the presentation
of these details that each work distinguishes itself. In The Last
Assembly Ball the central incidents are presented with blandish-
ments; Milly was legally married before she was abandoned, her
second lover-husband appeared unsolicited, and it was he who
ultimately committed suicide. Twenty-five years later, Foote's
depiction of Stella in A Picked Company is closer to that of Tess
than of Milly, though still less direct than the naturalistic manner
of her contemporaries Stephen Crane and Theodore Dreiser.

Like Hardy's Tess after Alec, Foote's Stella after Bradburn leads a promiscuous life; she too confesses her past to a different, virtuous young man who pledges his love. But whereas Tess "goes straight" at the end, having to murder Alec to do it, Stella is unregenerate, thus causing her lover's desperate action.

In the final analysis, *A Picked Company* is a story not of dissipation and destruction in the West but of the brave spirit and willing sacrifices made on the part of those who founded a permanent settlement on the frontier. In particular, Foote's tale of the Oregon migration leaves a lasting impression of the strength of the pioneer women who were part of the mission. None of the male characters is depicted with the force or feeling invested in Mrs. Hannington or in Stella, who between them represent the qualities most evident in the early female settlers. Bradburn implicitly draws the distinction between the two types when he lashes out at the men of Reverend Yardley's group:

"You lead about a wife, who is 'a believer'—fortunate for you. You put her in a log hut—God knows where! You expect her to bear you a child every two years and scrub the floor you pray on; she mends and makes, and saves, and teaches filthy Indians, and entertains all the travelling brothers and sisters, and adopts their orphans and keeps cheerful and faithful to the end. . . . Faith is like red hair; it goes with some temperaments, but every woman isn't born with that kind. You had a young lady with you that I am deeply attached to. Miss Mutrie could not live the life you expect your lawful wives to live. I wouldn't myself inflict such a life on a dog." (194–95)

As their names suggest, *Silence* Hannington represents the submissive "believer" who sacrifices earthly comfort to the demands of an exalted moral venture, while *Stella* is the starry-eyed infidel whose reckless vitality leads her to join the same journey. While Mrs. Hannington possesses the steadfast, oftimes inflexible New England character, Stella has the adventurous spirit that springs from a mixed heritage. Throughout the novel, Foote plays the two women of such differing natures against each other, sharpening the portrayal of each by antithesis. One is a quiet builder, the other a flamboyant gambler. The straightforward manner of Silence is symbolized by her rocking chair; the waywardness of Stella is conveyed through serpent imagery. The novel concludes with a tribute to Silence, and to all the emigrant women like her who endured and prevailed in the West:

Life to those pioneer women must have been heavily fraught with the restlessness and the melancholy that home memories breed; as the first years of marriage are haunted by memories of girlhood; as, all through life, we advance from one pioneer stage of experience to the next, attended by whisperings that clutch at our beating hearts out of the hearts which have ceased to beat in the countless generations that conducted us hither. (411)

In 1914, when these words were published, Mary Hallock Foote, aged sixty-seven, was very much aware of her status as a pioneer figure to the new generations; through the relentless passage of time, she was herself becoming a figure of the frontier past. For Arthur and Mary, the old order had begun to give way to the new. Death had diminished their circle: James Hague had died in 1908, Richard Watson Gilder the following year. Their children, meanwhile, had come of age: Betty was a wife of seven years and a mother; Arthur Burling had married and succeeded to his father's position at the North Star Mines. To Mary it was a new and interesting era, but one not altogether reassuring. For the first time in modern memory, the entire world was suddenly caught up by the senseless strife of war; it was no time, the pacifist told Helena, for an old lady to be writing.

CHAPTER 6

Achievement

IN 1915 Mary Hallock Foote saw through the press a novel, begun many years before, which she proclaimed would be her last. "No more," she wrote to Helena, "this could never have been written since the war."[1] She even commented in the novel's preface that it seemed strange "to be going on with mere mechanical revision—seated, as it were, with one's knitting at the spectacle of the world's agony since August of last year." Her shock and anguish at the present upheaval were genuine, but her commitment to the past so rapidly vanishing proved to be stronger. *The Valley Road* became not a valediction, but an overture: it represents the first of three realistic novels in which domestic fireside matters unfold against a backdrop of war. More significant, however, is that every work of this last, most successful phase of Foote's career is intensely autobiographical and honors the memory of a departed loved one. Freed from concern that the actual counterparts of her fictional figures would be recognized, Mary Hallock Foote published, between 1915 and 1919, three moving tributes to the past.

I The Valley Road

The Valley Road, a five-part chronicle of the Scarth family in Grass Valley between 1885 and 1906, is in part a fictionalized account of the relations between the Arthur Footes and the James D. Hagues. With the death of "J.D." in 1908, Mary lost a beloved and awesome brother-in-law and Arthur lost the man whose professional integrity and financial success had most bolstered his own. In her *Reminiscences* Mary commented that "if any man might successfully woo that coy lady, Eastern capital," it would be Hague; in *The Valley Road* she memorializes him as Thomas Ludwell ("T.L."), the San Francisco financier

139

who has "faith and capital and the nerve to stake much, if not all, with the courage to lose if his prophecies should fail."[2]

The novel opens in 1885, with Caroline Scarth giving birth to Engracia, her first child, in Massachusetts while Hal, her engineer-husband, is at work on the "Torresville Tract," a mining-irrigation scheme in California's Sacramento Valley. The following years are passed over until 1904, when the family's "story" really begins. The Scarth's son, Tom, is in Korea on an engineering project; Engracia, now nineteen, is at home; and Hal, past mid-life, is declining in health. As the summer approaches, Caroline, alarmed at her husband's condition and at her son's continued presence in the war zone, cables Tom to return. He makes the journey, unprepared for the "ambush of fate" awaiting him: the day that he arrives, his father dies after emergency surgery. Scarth's death brings the family closer to the Ludwells, their San Francisco relations, and causes significant changes.

During the summer, Tom assumes interim management of the Torresville project while Gifford Cornish, executor of the eastern man who had backed the scheme, journeys to California to determine the fate of the venture. Tom's promotion impresses his visiting cousin, Clare Ludwell, and she flirts with him, causing him to think less frequently of Mary, the American girl with whom he fell in love in Korea. After several weeks, however, Tom realizes that Clare actually loves a man from San Francisco, Dalby Morton, to whom she briefly becomes engaged. Engracia, too, makes a discovery of the heart: Cornish has fallen in love with her during his long business visit. The nineteen years' difference in their ages and the suddenness of his proposal make her decline, but Cornish remains loyal. He helps her, with reluctance, to obtain a position with his New York employer, Mrs. Rivington, widow of the man who financed Scarth's scheme.

It is against Caroline Scarth's best judgment to permit Engracia to become a social secretary, but the troubled family finances and her daughter's determination win the day. Within a year Engracia discovers why Cornish, who still writes her, was hesitant about her serving Mrs. Rivington: though the latter rejected Cornish's proposal of marriage many years before, she has begun to think of him affectionately since her husband's death. When the deluded widow confides to Engracia her plans

to marry Cornish, Engracia—appalled by the falsity around
her—breaks off communication with her suitor and flees Mrs.
Rivington, whose tissue of lies keeps Cornish baffled for months
about Engracia's turnabout.

In April 1906 the catastrophe of the San Francisco earthquake
proves a blessing for all the thwarted lovers. Tom is cabled by
Mary's mother in Korea to locate and assure the safety of her
daughter, who has been employed as a private nurse in the city;
Clare Ludwell returns from Europe with her parents to assess
the family losses; and Gifford Cornish travels from New York to
proffer financial aid to the stricken city. When Tom finds that
Mary is Dalby Morton's nurse, he invites the pair to exchange the
panic of the city for country quietude. Clare, now homeless,
comes to the Scarth residence also; and in little time she and
Dalby, and Mary and Tom, reach understandings. The latter pair
marry and depart for Korea, where Tom has received an offer of
employment. Clare and Dalby's attempted elopement is prevented, however, for Dalby, engaged to another, must extricate
himself honorably before a wedding can take place.

The novel closes with the marriage of Engracia and Cornish
and with Caroline Scarth, pleased with the matches of her
children, ending her western exile and returning to the home of
her childhood to live with Olivia, her maiden cousin. Though she
has received similar invitations from both her son and daughter,
she has wisely declined:

And it cost her no great pang in one way, for she wanted silence and
peace; and if there should be problems in these young lives they were
not her problems;—and she could not at her time of life bring to a new
set of problems the courage she had brought to her own. Nor does the
understanding of one generation fit the needs of the next. No; she
wanted to lie at anchor in some quiet haven and dream her own dreams
and think over her life—with him. And more than art or clothes or
clever talk, though she had loved these things in her youth, did she love
her personal life apart, the solitude she had grown used to and learned
to need;—room for the lonely soul which each of us must bring to our
last account with life, in preparation for what we trust will come after.
(352-53)

This final passage, marked by a shift from Caroline Scarth's
point of view to that of Mary Hallock Foote, is one of the few

indications within the novel of Foote's inability to distance
herself from the story she created. The fictional situation of *The
Valley Road*—that of a woman's sudden bereavement and her
subsequent vicarious existence through her children—was close,
perhaps too close, to Foote's own experience; but even her best
friend did not fully recognize this. Writing to congratulate Foote
on the publication of her tenth novel, Helena reminded her that
Richard had earlier published a poem by the same title. Foote's
disavowal—"It is strange (and very sweet to me) about the name.
It must have lain in the back of my memory unconnected
absolutely with its source."[3]—was genuine, for *The Valley Road*
seems not to have been inspired by any particular literary work.
It represents, rather, a blend of incidents from the author's
experience and imagination.

Though the Scarth's "Roadside" is not a recreation of North
Star House, its proximity to Marysville, California, pinpoints the
Grass Valley setting. The details of Caroline Scarth's family life
in Massachusetts are those of Mary Hallock's girlhood: the
maiden widowhood of Cousin Olivia (Cousin Anna Haviland,
Mary's namesake), Engracia's christening (Arthur Burling's),
Cornish's arrival and Engracia's home wedding (Arthur and
Mary's). The Torresville scheme is reminiscent of the Idaho
project,[4] complete to the untimely death of the backer and the
visit of the stockholders' representative. The accounts of the
Ludwell generosity and prosperity correspond to the Hagues'
position, but other details are fictional, particularly the Clare-
Dalby subplot which culminates in a thwarted elopement
reminiscent of that in "A Touch of Sun." The wholly fictional
scenes of the tempestuous love affairs within the Scarth and
Ludwell families involve numerous strained coincidences; but
the device of the earthquake increases their plausibility, with
the postquake chaos reflecting the domestic upheaval.

In the final analysis, it is manner, not content, which
distinguishes the novel. The overall effect achieved is one of
understated intensity. As one reviewer observed, commenting on
the story's "delicate force," Foote "possessed herself of the thing
called style at a time when it was rather highly valued."[5] What
The Valley Road reflects is an ease, an "unlabored care" absent
from many of the author's earlier novels. Always scrupulous,
Mary Hallock Foote invested considerable effort in framing and
polishing what she thought would be her final production.

II   Edith Bonham

In 1916 Helena Gilder died, and Mary Hallock Foote, guided by sure instinct of the rightness of her tribute, began a novel to honor the person who had represented "the strongest influence my life has known outside of its daily companions of flesh and blood."[6] Published in 1917 and dedicated to Helena, *Edith Bonham* is Foote's only work titled for its heroine and presented from her perspective. Like *The Valley Road*, the novel is, in part, drawn from Foote's life, yet it is a more skillful conversion of autobiography into fiction. It is presented, ingeniously, as though it were from Helena's point of view: Edith (Helena) bequeaths her diary to the daughter of Nanny Maclay. Through the device of Edith's diary, the story of the artistic New Yorker's deep devotion for Nanny (Molly), her quiet friend from up the Hudson, is told.

The "marriage of true minds" between the girls, so perfect at first, is threatened one summer by Nanny's sudden betrothal and marriage to a man who takes her West. Edith finds Nanny unbearably unfamiliar as Mrs. Douglas Maclay, wife of an Idaho mining and irrigation engineer, until the latter makes her first return visit East. The two resume their closeness, and Edith—who develops a deep affection for Nanny's daughter Phoebe and who senses Nanny's isolation in the West—resolves to befriend her by a singularly self-sacrificing act. She pledges to join the Maclays in Idaho as a companion-governess when their infant daughter is of suitable age.[7]

Four years later the arrangement is ready to be effected, and the maidenly Edith, now twenty-seven-years old, travels to Boise only to learn on arrival that Nanny has died following the birth of a son. Shocked and griefstricken, she is assured by Maclay that her services are needed more than ever, and she determines to honor her promise. With aid from Maclay's household staff and from his assistant, Dick Grant, "Aunt Edith" soon restores a normal routine and wins the affection of Phoebe. Nanny's image is ever present to Edith as she selflessly buries her own life, but her idealized vision of a household devoted to her friend's memory is shattered when Grant proposes to her. Surmising that he was earlier in love with Nanny, she firmly declines, shocked by the general inconstancy of men.

A greater concern becomes hers, however, when Phoebe

contracts scarlet fever. Edith flees with her young charge to an isolated house built on a mesa in the Boise valley; there, with frequent visits from Maclay, she keeps a quarantine vigil. At the end of six weeks, with Phoebe's health restored, Edith is stunned anew when Maclay asks her to become his wife. Embittered that the memory of Nanny, gone but four months, should be so quickly desecrated, Edith refuses. When she returns to Boise she comes to realize that Maclay was offering her protection in the only way he knew, for her unchaperoned status has occasioned vicious gossip. But this does not ease her hurt, and with relief she soon escapes by accepting the invitation of Nanny's parents to bring the grandchildren and make her home with them.

On arrival at their Hudson Valley farm, she readily submerges herself in the routine concerns of caring for Phoebe and her young brother. More than five years pass, during which she hears from Maclay only through his letters to Phoebe. Though she can read, between the lines, of his continuing love for her, she is too proud to signal that she has relented. In the interim Dick Grant visits and tells her of his own coming marriage, while Nanny's mother, divining the impasse between Edith and Maclay, urges her son-in-law to visit. He arrives, the two reconcile and marry, and Edith returns to the West.

Having studiously avoided the clichés of the governess-widower formula, Mary Hallock Foote concludes the novel with an afterword by Phoebe, who comments on her stepmother's diary and remarks on the changes since Edith's death (significantly, World War I). Though these "Last Words" strike the reader as anticlimactic, they are the author's device for rendering homage to the real-life friend to whom she had once confessed, "The touches of unworthiness have always been on my side"[8]:

That was Aunt Edith—"mother," queen of all mothers, perfect in love, in friendship, in magnanimity, the soul of friendship, which came as natural to her as vanity and selfishness to smaller natures.

It is not for me to discuss them, to take stock of their different qualities and capabilities—my two mothers, now that both are gone. Each would have shrunk from the thought of such comparison. But I know that my own mother would have said that her friend was incomparably the greater person—and for herself she would have asked no praise beyond the fact: "Edith loved me as I am."[9]

In a less conspicuous manner, the novel is also a tribute to two of the men in Foote's life. In Dick Grant, the "Young Hermes" with "fair hair close-waved about the temples that were wingless" (95), she recreates the handsome figure of Harry Tompkins, who had shared with her the pain and disappointment of the Idaho scheme. Tompkins had passed away in 1914; it was safe, now, to fictionalize the nature of his ordeal in Idaho:

> It had not taken any time at all to recognize *his* trouble, as old as the hills. Perhaps Nanny never knew it. She was preoccupied, and Dick had fine qualities at his command. He might have been unselfish enough never to let her see it. It took me back to her tale of the mesa—lonely little chatelaine on her dry hill; "hands," men of all sorts, and four-footed beasts raising a dust around her and all the good money in the ground spent in vain. Dick must have been older than he looked, for he had been out there, part of and witness of all she endured. No wonder he had loved her. And, I added to myself, no wonder a reader of men, as a "good boss" must be, had trusted him. But she was the one who must have quite unconsciously decided the course of that perilous partnership. (96)

Like Grant, Tompkins had at one point brought his fiancée to meet the woman whom he had adored in Idaho, and Foote had rejoiced in his happiness. She rejoiced, too, that there had been nothing to conceal from her husband about their friendship. For it is Arthur, alias Douglas Maclay, who provides the story's power and tension. It is as if Foote wished Helena to see Arthur as she herself saw him, to explain to her friend, as she had tried in 1874, that "the human heart in its natural workings is the most mysterious thing in the world."[10] In the protracted struggle of wills between Edith and Douglas, it is Douglas who triumphs and who wins Edith's respect as well as her love.

In a larger sense, the novel is Foote's vindication not only of Arthur but of the West he symbolized. Edith, of the "gay, arrogant, worldly Bonhams" (257) has been raised amidst New York's fascinating artist colony and has traveled extensively, yet she chooses ultimately to make her life in the land of sunshine and shadow. As she explains to her incredulous sister, the West has a "haunting" power, a "tremendous force, concealed somehow; things may happen any time, but you don't know what, nor where to expect them" (236). Later, in Phoebe's "Last

Words," Foote offers a defense of the Boise area where she had once felt imprisoned, thus making peace with the past. At seventy, the author no longer felt the despair of thirty or the rancor of forty. The West had become "her" West: from *The Led-Horse Claim* (1881), where the forcing nature of the western experience causes the well-bred eastern hero to kill a man and live the rest of his days under the shadow of that tragedy, to *The Prodigal* (1901), where the eastern hero with a tarnished past redeems himself in the West, to *Edith Bonham* (1917), where the eastern heroine freely chooses to live out her life in the West and finds her greatest happiness there—the process of emotional acceptance and literary assimilation had become complete. Through the guise of fiction, Foote sought in *Edith Bonham* to affirm her own commitment and that of those closest to her; the novel offers reassurance that life can be lived in the West without compromise to one's integrity and vision.

III   The Ground-Swell

In the latter months of 1919, as she was approaching seventy-two years of age, Mary Hallock Foote published her twelfth and final novel. Like its immediate predecessor, *The Ground-Swell* is concerned with the parent-child relationship viewed from a mother's perspective; the first-person narrative takes the form of the mother's correspondence to her closest friend. The time is the twelve-month period following June 1914, when the world stood aghast at the mounting fury of war. For Lucy Cope and her husband Charles, a retired general in the army, a summer camping vacation along the northern California shoreline becomes the occasion for introspection and discovery. The Copes come to realize that the ground swells they watch—the deep ocean swells occasioned by disturbances far out at sea—symbolize the disorder within and without their coastal world.

The Copes devote much of their vacation at Laguna Point seeking a suitable site for their last home where, they hope, their youngest daughter Katherine will also come to live. The latter is a social worker in New York; her older, married sisters are Patty, stationed with her army husband in the Philippines, and Cecily, married to a wealthy San Francisco socialite named Peter Dalbert. When Katherine arrives at Laguna Point for a visit, her mother introduces her to Tony Kayding, caretaker of the coastal ranch on which they are camping. Mrs. Cope secretly hopes that Kayding will win her daughter over, but Katherine is a "modern girl" who has pledged her energies and sympathies to the cause of orphan relief. She professes herself too deeply involved with her social work to renounce it for marriage.

During Katherine's stay, Mrs. Cope also establishes contact with Cecily, from whom she receives a despairing account of Peter's dissipation and philandering. She even unexpectedly witnesses, at Laguna Point, her son-in-law's assignation with a disreputable woman, their quarrel, and his cowardice in not preventing the woman's fatal fall to the ocean below. The shocked Mrs. Cope warns Peter that she will divulge to others the details of this repugnant incident and will urge Cecily to seek a divorce unless he cleanses himself through honest labor and a trial separation. Then, relinquishing all hope of building a home, the disillusioned matron readily assents to her husband's proposal that they go East for the winter:

It was a time of transition and suspense, and states of mind—because we didn't know the ground under our feet. The war—which we did not talk of—kept my husband in a fever, as I knew; I was nervous on his account. And the spreading peril abroad seemed reflected microscopically in our own family affairs. . . . We were transfixed, both nationally and individually, in a nightmare of helplessness.[11]

In New York, Mrs. Cope resumes a close relationship with Katherine and recognizes that the latter will never marry Kayding; instead, with the escalation of aggression in Europe, Katherine soon departs for France to join the war effort. Peter Dalbert, seizing the opportunity as a means of penance, also goes abroad to serve. The Copes are drawn back to California when Kayding, who has become heir to the vast land he served as overseer, offers General Cope the position of ranch manager. On her return, Mrs. Cope is surprised to discover that a house has been built at Laguna Point. Unsuspecting to the end, she learns from Kayding that the home is to be her own private haven, her shelter from the ground swells of life. The novel ends with General Cope being recalled to active duty, and with the news that Katherine has died in France, mysteriously, from an attack of grippe:[12]

Her death, we say to each other, was not a mistake, it was a necessity of her previous life and her whole attitude toward life; and it was that in her which counted. She lost no time. . . . And now that she is gone there is no more to say about us as a family: Patty's story has scarcely begun; Cecy's pauses till Peter comes back; Tony is committed to his chosen work, and Katherine's work is done. (279-80)

The Ground-Swell was inspired by the Footes' 1915 summer vacation at Pescadero Point, south of San Francisco. Mary, anxious about the war, wrote Helena that the site was beautiful but appropriately stormy: "Never was the world in such a perilous pass, and one could brood on it night and day. . . . All day and all night 'the grey sky is over us,' and the crashing of waves on the rocks and beaches and the 'long drawn thunder' down the shores."[13] Amidst this tempestuous setting she subsequently developed the delicate figure of Katherine Cope, to whom much of the story's attention is given. Her character derives in part from Arthur's sister Katherine, who had insisted she was "not a marrying man" and had followed a successful career in New York; but primarily she is Agnes, the beloved daughter for whom Foote wished to write a memorial. Endowed with lightness of spirit and steadfastness of purpose, Katherine makes The Ground-Swell come alive. At times, in her relationship with Kayding, she is a figure of romance, likened to Tennyson's Lynette testing Gareth; sometimes she is "Amy," whom the master of Locksley Hall can neither forget nor comprehend. But most of the while she is a young woman whose exuberance for living and strong humanitarian commitment inspire those around her.

The emotional and intellectual distance between Katherine Cope, Foote's last heroine, and Cecil Conrath, her first, is a measure of the change in women's roles which Mary Hallock Foote witnessed during her long writing career. Cecil, the "protected woman" who visits Leadville and is unexpectedly caught up in a mining controversy, is the late nineteenth-century female of convention: she shuns involvement, flees to safety, and accepts as suitor one who will create for her a refuge from the world. She is, as Foote commented many years after creating her, a "silly sort of heroine. . . . Yet girls were like that, 'lots of them,' in my time."[14] Katherine, with her cool self-sufficiency and skepticism of tradition, represents Cecil's antithesis: she is an arch-realist who confronts life without illusions. Until her untimely death, she is very much influenced by her close friendship with the "brilliant" woman who first aroused her interest in orphan relief. The two belong to a circle of "third-sex" women, as the bewildered Mrs. Cope terms them, who suppress their femininity and replace it with commitment to an idea. It is Katherine's devotion to her friend Helen, and to Helen's cause, which takes her to France and costs her her life.

Katherine Cope is thus a type of young woman conspicuously absent from Foote's previous fiction, a type whose omission the author had confessed to more than thirty years before:

> My girls never have a "career"; never do anything to advance the "causes"; have not the missionary spirit; do not show any progressive spirit even as towards "man.". . . To be honest, I am a sad recreant in these matters of woman's place in the future—the near future:—in politics and the professions, and in everything conspicuously progressive.[15]

That Mary Hallock Foote, Victorian gentlewoman, should in her final novel draw such a sympathetic portrait of the emerging modern woman is testimony to her literary skill, and tribute to the independent spirit of the daughter she had lost.

In all respects, *The Ground-Swell* offers evidence of its author's talents at their best. The presentation of the unhurried life on the western shore and its frenzied counterpart in the East; the contrasts between Mrs. Cope's maternal concerns, Katherine's selfless cares, and Cecily's materialistic desires; and the connecting links between the uncertainties of love and war are all firmly drawn. In depicting the delicate relations between generations and in presenting them from the vantage of her own wisdom born of experience, Foote's literary touch is surest: along with *The Desert and the Sown* and *Edith Bonham, The Ground-Swell* ranks as her finest novel. All three are written in the realistic mode; two are first-person narratives, with the point of view employed so effectively that one concludes the author should have utilized first person more frequently during her career. The novels are noteworthy not for their action but for their study of human character. Emily Bogardus, Edith Bonham, and Lucy Cope—three mothers struggling to guide their children, three women with close ties to both the East and the West—emerge as finely wrought, psychologically complex figures. It is they who provide the background against which the actions of the younger generation are played; it is their maternal concerns which serve as the rationale for each story. Written by an author approaching and then well into her sixties, the novels offer fine evidence of Foote's literary resiliency.

IV   Reminiscences

After *The Ground-Swell* the public voice of Mary Hallock Foote ceased to be heard, the author professing that her era was over. Literature, she confided to those around her, was the province of the new generation of writers, of Willa Cather and Anne Douglas Sedgwick, whose work she admired so much.[16] The distance between the fiction emerging during the twenties, and her own work published years before, she was able to measure with accuracy: the vogue of genteel romance, and of realism tempered by reticence, had passed away. Yet judging from the literary notices which continued to be published, there were many who hoped that Foote's silence was only temporary. Devoting a newspaper column in 1923 to the Quaker author who had "long been nationally recognized as an important novelist," Eric Howard observed: "For thirty-six years, from 1883 to 1919, she has lived quietly and written thoughtful, interesting stories of her unusual experiences. One hopes that still more stories will come from her pen, for her work is a distinctive contribution to the literature of California and the West."[17]

Relatives prevailed upon Foote successfully, at last, to undertake a final literary project—her autobiography. She began "Backgrounds with Figures," as it was tentatively titled, in the early 1920s and worked on it, intermittently, to mid-decade. Though reluctant to submit her manuscript for publication, she sent a fragment to one journal and it was declined.[18] After that the manuscript remained in variant versions within the family but was brought forward for publication decades later through the offices of her granddaughters and great nephew. Under the expert editing of Rodman Paul, Mary Hallock Foote's *Reminiscences* became available in book form in 1972. Written when she was nearing eighty, the autobiography represents an impressive capstone to her literary career.

Foote had told Helena Gilder in 1894, when the latter was preparing for publication her laudatory review of Mary as an artist-author, that "to tell the truth about one's self, I believe, is next to impossible." For Foote, the more the past receded, the more idealized it became—and, as Rodman Paul has noted, the more anxious she was to bury painful memories. Her autobiography thus evidences the way in which the passage of time softens perspective and gives form to experience. Though the *Reminiscences* begin, chronologically, with the facts of her parentage and infancy, Foote makes no attempt to present a balanced account of the life that followed: small incidents are magnified, others muted, long periods are blurred and softened. At one point she comments, "These fragments of my past are presented merely as backgrounds and the figures upon them are placed by instinct in a selected light and seen from a certain point of view. To that extent I suppose I am still the artist I tried to be, and the old romancer too."[19] In other words, her account is suggestive rather than revealing: her private correspondence is necessary companion reading for one interested in fact as well as art.

The extent to which Foote exercises literary license is determinable from the space accorded various eras of her life. She underscores the influence of her Quaker childhood, devoting over one-fifth of her narrative to the years before her marriage; and she stresses the excursion to Mexico, devoting a disproportionate amount of space to an experience of less than four months. The twelve years in Idaho are accorded little more space than the earlier stays in California and Colorado, which lasted but half as long. The Grass Valley era of more than thirty years comprises the briefest section of all. As Foote writes in the concluding chapter, "I once thought that when I was done writing stories I would take the stories that have been lived on the North Star Surface for a theme, but I have waited too long: I know it all too well; its roots are too deep in my own life in these thirty years we have lived here" (394).

What Foote is obliquely admitting is that she cannot effectively distance herself from the tragedy which occurred at Grass Valley in 1904. In the sense that her final years were grounded in the tragedy of Agnes's death, she bears comparison with her contemporary Mark Twain,[20] whose *Autobiography* frequently comes to mind as one reads the *Reminiscences*. The Milton Quaker and the Hannibal humorist both conclude their own remarkable stories not with an account of the blessings that wisdom and maturity confer but with an abrupt ending—a dramatic description of loss. For Foote as for Twain, the untimely death of a beloved daughter robbed the subsequent years of their significance. Like Twain, Foote is content to leave the rest to silence:

All that has happened here since [Agnes's death] would be too difficult to tell for one so deeply implicated through her relations to the chief actors, yet so powerless, as myself. . . . History must pause. But the North Star House now has its own flock of children, little Californians to whom this place will always be home; its memories will haunt them as the desert wind and the sound of that cañon river rising to our windows at night has stayed with our own children all their lives. (399)

With its panoramic subject—embracing both coasts of the continent and spanning the era from before the Civil War to past the turn of the century—Foote's life is the stuff of which drama is made, as has been superbly demonstrated by Wallace Stegner's *Angle of Repose* (1971) and by the opera *Angle of Repose*, based on Stegner's novel and first performed in 1976. Yet equaling the force of either of these imaginative versions is the life itself as Foote relates it in the *Reminiscences*. From the quiet milldams of Milton to the noisy mining stamps of Leadville, from the marital and professional disappointments of the Idaho period to the comforts and acclaim of the early Grass Valley years—this personal account of a woman "irretrievably married into the West" makes compelling reading. The *Reminiscences* amply demonstrate Foote's talents to absorb and recreate the details of a scene, to transmute unusual incident into memorable expression, and to discern the substance of human behavior as well as its effect. Pervading all is a keen sense of atmosphere—of light and setting, heightening and selection—with the harshness of reality ever softened and filtered. To read Mary Hallock Foote's story is to return to a bygone era, recreated from "the magic perspectives of memory."

Foote's autobiography has genuine distinction whether judged as a literary endeavor or as a document of historical and antiquarian interest. More enlightening and far better written than most of the published letters and diaries of other nineteenth-century women drawn to the western frontier,[21] it is best judged in relation to the memoirs of other authors. In particular, the productions of two fellow New Yorkers are logical candidates for comparison: Caroline Kirkland's *A New Home*—

Who'll Follow? (1839) and Edith Wharton's *A Backward Glance,* written during the early 1930s and published in 1934. Like Foote, Kirkland had been Quaker educated, had journeyed to the frontier (Michigan) upon marriage, and had subsequently written romances and short fiction. Her autobiography, one of her earlier works, is romanticized: as she explained in the preface, "I must honestly confess, that there be glosses, and colorings, and lights, if not shadows, for which the author is alone accountable."[22] A reading of *A New Home,* however, reveals neither the exactness of locale nor beauty of phrase which characterizes Foote's *Reminiscences.* In sustained interest, as well, Kirkland's work pales in comparison.

A *Backward Glance,* on the other hand, is as finished a production as Foote's, but less understated. Like Foote, Wharton was periodically beset by uncertainty about her roles as wife and literary artist, and she reveals these doubts more directly. Too, her autobiography becomes a showcase for exhibiting the many celebrated authors whose friendship she enjoyed, while Foote's work focuses rather on portraits of family. Despite these outward differences, however, the *Reminiscences* read well when compared with Wharton's famous work. In coming years, as Foote's recently published autobiography wins new readers, it will probably be judged her most enduring literary accomplishment.

Several years after the completion of the *Reminiscences,* Mary and Arthur, "professional exiles" for more than five decades, returned to the East to spend the last phase of their lives. With Betty and her family, they lived peacefully in Hingham, Massachusetts, until death claimed Arthur in 1933.[23] Mary survived him by almost five years, dying on June 25, 1938, five months before her ninety-first birthday.[24] Even in her final years she was an engaging figure, as her granddaughter, Janet Foote Micoleau, has affirmed:

I remember her as a charming, animated little person, with an almost girlish air of shyness. She blushed easily, kept her eyes cast down a great deal of the time (partly, I think, because they were sensitive to bright light) and had a way of covering her face with her hands when she laughed. She was, however, a great talker and, when with stimulating people, would often get "carried away" and would groan with shame afterward at having "talked too much." But her conversation was never dull. Her life had been interesting, and she was witty and well-read, with an extraordinary memory which enabled her to quote liberally from her favorite authors. . . . When other grandmothers wore short skirts, bobbed hair and permanents, she wore skirts to her ankles and white caps in the Quaker tradition over hair, which had never turned grey but had become very thin. She also followed the Quaker custom of using "thee" instead of "you" when talking to members of the family.

That Mary Hallock Foote's unassuming personality remained unchanged through the years is a tribute to her early upbringing in the Quaker household by the Hudson. Though her achievements had brought her fame and distinction even into the twentieth century, she had the humility to recognize her limitations and to promote the abilities of the new generation. As one who visited her in the 1930s recalled, Mary Hallock Foote possessed "surprising understanding and toleration of the foibles of the present era," but remained herself "an exquisite gentlewoman of an era now closed."[25]

CHAPTER 7

Assessment

HAD Mary Hallock Foote developed only her faculty for illustration, and never tried writing at all, she would still have merited recognition beyond her lifetime. Remarkable though it was that a woman of her genteel background would choose to pursue a career, it was all the more notable that her black-and-white drawings were among the very best of those produced when American illustration enjoyed its heyday. Judging from the considerable artistic progress she made within a decade of her commercial debut in the late 1860s, there seems little doubt that her talent was still developing when, in 1881, she shifted her focus and energies to literature. By 1895, when she had virtually ceased illustrating, her work was considered on a par with that of the very best practitioners of the day— persons like Howard Pyle, Frederic Remington, Joseph Pennell, and Thomas Moran, whose fame as illustrators continues to the present day. One suspects that had Foote not been a woman in a man's profession, and had she not retired early from the field, her credentials as a leading nineteenth-century illustrator would need no introduction.

Since her skill as an illustrator won her friendships with many of the leading authors and prominent editors of the time, Foote might have remained in the East, "in free access to the educated circles of the day," as Rodman Paul has observed. Instead, she chose to follow a man whose career took her from one part of the rapidly vanishing frontier to another. As she discovered that Western scenes were suited to her artist's pencil, and that her epistolary accounts of the West were warmly received by friends, it was natural, given her considerable talent, that she should turn from illustrating the works of others to authoring and illustrating tales about her new region.

From the very beginning of her literary career, her central

155

concern was to explore the impact of the Far West upon those whose homeland it became. Thus for Foote, one continuing artistic problem was that of effectively distancing her material from her own situation. Just as in her personal life she moved gradually from disaffection to wholehearted participation in western life, so as an author she struggled to achieve the stance of a sensitive, discerning observer. Her early tales of heroines sacrificed needlessly to the demands of the West were too closely intertwined with her own personal dissatisfactions to be good art. The better work came later, once she had accepted her residency in the West as permanent. It was then that she strove for and achieved what she called "the true note" unblunted by "the alien touch."[1]

The other artistic problem which too often limited the range of Foote's work was her penchant for the romance. Given the freshness of her western material and the vogue of local-color literature after the Civil War, it is surprising that Foote did not follow the course adopted by so many other authors, and, in particular, by so many female authors. Yet with the exception of a handful of tales—among which are "The Story of the Alcázar" and "How the Pump Stopped at the Morning Watch," her best short fictions—she bears little comparison with contemporaries like Mary Austin, who also wrote of the Far West, or with eastern local colorists like Sarah Orne Jewett or Mary Wilkins Freeman. For twenty years Foote seldom departed from the romance formula which her editors sanctioned and her readers enjoyed. Like Cooper and Stevenson, whose works she emulated, she substituted sensitivity for exploitation and succeeded in making her chosen region a subject of interest and romance; yet her heavy dependence upon conventional love stories prevented her from finding an adequate form for her western experience. Only after the turn of the century did she learn to balance her predilection for romance with the demands of realism. Her final production, though autobiography rather than fiction, represents a masterful blend of the two, while The Desert and the Sown, Edith Bonham, and The Ground Swell—late works written in the realistic vein—are her best novels. Though a romancer by nature, she was shrewd enough to discover that her material was better suited to realistic treatment, and she was a craftsman of sufficient competence to make the transition successfully.

It is the dichotomy between East and West which gives

complexity and form to Foote's work. All her fiction is given to exploring the forces represented by these two—the refined power of the East and the unharnessed energy of the West. Again and again the elements are reexamined and renamed, but always contrasted: East versus West, past versus future, art versus love, security versus adventure, the ideal versus the actual. Foote's first work, "The Picture in the Fire-place Bedroom," and early productions like "The Fate of a Voice" and "Pilgrims to Mecca" pit allegiance to the cultural achievements of the East against the pull of romantic and familial ties already established in the West. In subsequent fictions, there is an increasing acceptance of the West on its own terms. Whereas in *The Led-Horse Claim* and *John Bodewin's Testimony* the East stands for moral security while the West represents instability, in late novels such as *The Valley Road* and *The Ground-Swell* exactly the reverse is true: the East is insecure, the West, a haven. Similarly, in the early works such as *The Led-Horse Claim* and *The Last Assembly Ball,* Foote emphasizes the discrepancy between societal standards as they are upheld in the East and as they are ineffectually practiced in the West—the difference, in other words, between the ideal and the actual. But in *The Desert and the Sown* and *Edith Bonham,* such values are reversed: the West becomes the ideal, symbolizing fertility and regeneration in contrast to eastern sterility. Foote's evolving attitude toward the West thus lends credence to Owen Wister's remark that hers was the first voice "lifted to honor the cattle country and not to libel it."[2]

For more than four decades Mary Hallock Foote successfully confronted the arduous and relentless demands of authorship, and her works reflect both the pitfalls and the triumphs of such a sustained endeavor. For the modern reader the deficiencies of Foote's writing lie primarily in the excessively idealized characters, romantic situations, and moral tone of her early fiction. Her frequent reliance upon coincidence and melodrama, her pointedly symbolic naming of many characters, and her excessive dependence upon two or three formalized plots are further shortcomings. Yet her work after 1895—the fiction written after her initial alienation and after the disappointment and strain of the Idaho years—demonstrates a general excellence, for it is at this point that she achieves maturity of style and perspective. Her command of atmosphere becomes remarkable, with her

keen eye for setting consorting with her faculty for description
to produce many exceptional passages. The deathbed scenes of
the pumpman in "Morning Watch" and of John Hagar Bogardus
in *The Desert and the Sown* are particularly fine. Characterization, too, is a forte of her later writing, with her figures —
particularly female — achieving a remarkable humanness. Silence
Hannington and Stella Mutrie, Emily Bogardus and Lucy Cope —
each remains vividly etched in the reader's memory. And gracing
most of the later work is a delicacy and deftness of style that
alone would make the reading rewarding.

Throughout her literary career Mary Hallock Foote made no
pretensions to greatness, was modest about excellence when she
achieved it, and was cognizant of the unusual external circumstances which sometimes impeded her accomplishments. As she
set about converting into literature her firsthand observations of
frontier life and her varied experiences in the Far West, she
neither attempted to provide a philosophical commentary upon
the human condition nor — with the exception of one novel,
Coeur d'Alene — to champion particular ideas. Rather, she
approached her material without dogmatism, looking upon it, as
her best friend remarked, "with the large gaze of an artist, a
woman, and a sensitive but not a sentimental or sensational
writer."[3] Though hers was not among the greater voices heard in
American literature between 1880-1925, she is by no means a
figure to be forgotten. As a highly accomplished chronicler and
illustrator of a significant bygone era, Mary Hallock Foote
deserves a secure place in American letters.

Notes and References

All letters cited from Mary Hallock Foote (MHF) are at Stanford University Library unless otherwise noted.

Preface

1. *Selected American Prose, 1841–1900: The Realistic Movement,* ed. with Introduction by Wallace Stegner (New York, 1958), p. xi.

Chapter One

1. From an unpublished autobiographical fragment entitled "Foreword," transcribed by George McMurry (courtesy of Stanford University Library).

2. From an unpublished autobiographical fragment entitled "The People Called in Scorn, Quakers," transcribed by George McMurry (courtesy of Stanford University Library).

3. *A Victorian Gentlewoman in the Far West: The Reminiscences of Mary Hallock Foote,* ed. Rodman W. Paul (San Marino, Calif., 1972), p. 195—hereafter cited as *Reminiscences* (quoted with permission of the Henry E. Huntington Library). Foote's previous description of her mother is quoted by Regina Armstrong, "Representative American Women Illustrators," *Critic* 37 (August 1900): 138.

4. *Reminiscences,* pp. 5, 51–52.

5. Ibid., p. 54.

6. "The People Called in Scorn, Quakers" (courtesy of Stanford University Library).

7. Mary Hallock lived in the Ellwood Walter home on Columbia Street. So desirable was Walter's bayside location that John Roebling, chief engineer for the construction of the Brooklyn Bridge, purchased the home when Walter moved in 1865. At that time Mary moved to the home of her uncle, V. H. Hallock, in Valley Stream, Long Island.

8. Helena de Kay Gilder, "Author Illustrators, II: Mary Hallock Foote," *Book Buyer* 11 (August 1894): 338.

9. Francis B. Smith, *Radical Artisan: William J. Linton* (Manchester, England, 1973), p. 159.

10. Gilder, *Book Buyer,* pp. 339–40. The previous description of Foote—in a letter of July 18, 1955, from Janet Foote Micoleau, her

159

granddaughter, to Mary Lou Benn—is published in Benn's article "Mary Hallock Foote: Early Leadville Writer," *Colorado Magazine* 33 (April 1956): 108. Foote permitted her picture to be published only twice during her lifetime: see Gilder, *Book Buyer*, p. 338, and Charles F. Lummis, "The New League for Literature and the West," *Land of Sunshine* 8 (April 1898): 208.

11. Foote's remark is quoted by Alpheus Sherwin Cody, "Artist-Authors," *Outlook* 49 (May 26, 1894): 911.

12. See MHF to the Knickerbocker Publishing Company, April 9, 1906 (courtesy of the State Historical Society of Wisconsin). William Rimmer (1816-1879) was principal of the School of Design and taught black-and-white illustration. William J. Linton (1812-1897), distinguished artist and author of *The Masters of Wood Engraving*, taught drawing and engraving. In his article "The History of Wood-Engraving in America: Part IV," *American Art and American Art Collections*, ed. Walter Montgomery (Boston, 1889), I, 469-70, Linton honored MHF by including two of her illustrations. Foote's unceasing admiration for Linton is evident in *Reminiscences.*

13. Mary Hallock to Helena de Kay, undated [c. July 1867]. The Foote-Gilder correspondence, deposited at Stanford University Library, is hereafter cited as MH to HdK or, when appropriate, as MHF to HG.

14. *Reminiscences*, pp. 86-87. For her illustrations, see Albert Deane Richardson, *Beyond the Mississippi* (Hartford, Conn., 1867), pp. 357, 483, 488, 516.

15. The quotation is taken from Elizabeth Robins Pennell, *The Life and Letters of Joseph Pennell* (Boston, 1929), I, 39. Linton's comment appears in "History of Wood-Engraving," p. 464.

16. Joseph Pennell (1857-1926), a highly successful American artist-illustrator, is perhaps best known for his illustrations of the novels of G. W. Cable, Henry James, and W. D. Howells. E. A. Abbey (1852-1911) achieved fame with his illustrations of Shakespeare's plays.

17. MH to HG, undated [c. fall 1874].

18. *Reminiscences*, p. 102.

19. W. D. Howells, "Recent Literature," *Atlantic Monthly* 34 (December 1874): 745-46.

20. A. V. S. Anthony to HG, undated [c. August 1894]. The Whittier comment is quoted in Samuel T. Pickard, *Life and Letters of John Greenleaf Whittier* (Boston and New York, 1894), II, 599.

21. John Burroughs, "Picturesque Aspects of Farm Life in New York," *Scribner's Monthly* 17 (November 1878): 41, passim. See also "On the Ice," *Hearth and Home* 5 (January 18, 1873): cover. Lathrop's remark appears in his review "Art," *Atlantic Monthly* 37 (February 1876): 251.

22. *Reminiscences*, p. 103, 100-101. Elihu Vedder (1836-1923)

achieved fame as an author and illustrator with his illustrations for the
Rubáiyát of Omar Khayyam (1883-84). Kate Bloede, one of Foote's
classmates at Cooper, married the artist Abbott Thayer (1849-1921).
Ehrman S. Nadal (1843-1922) wrote *Impressions of London Social Life*
(1875).

23. Clark C. Spence, *Mining Engineers and the American West* (New
Haven, Conn., 1970), pp. 1-2.

24. MH to HdK, December 1873.

25. "The Picture in the Fire-place Bedroom," *St. Nicholas Magazine*
2 (February 1875): 248-50. Cf. the description of the room of Foote's
grandmother, Mrs. Burling, in *Reminiscences*, p. 108. Foote's tale seems
a conscious tribute to the enduring values represented by Mrs. Burling,
who died in 1868.

26. *Reminiscences*, pp. 105-06. The ceremony was attended by
family and a few close friends, including Richard Watson Gilder.
Helena, recovering from the birth of the Gilders' first child in January,
remained in New York City.

27. *Reminiscences*, p. 114. Foote's letter to Helena is dated June 18,
1876.

Chapter Two

1. From an unpublished manuscript fragment entitled "Introduction" (courtesy of Stanford University Library).

2. Mary Hague is quoted in MHF to HG, January 1878.

3. *Reminiscences*, pp. 129-30.

4. W. D. Howells, "Recent Fiction," *Atlantic Monthly* 40 (December 1877): 753.

5. That the essay is a pastiche is evident from Foote's letter of
September 29, 1877, to the Gilders: "It is too bad for you to spend so
much time, your own precious time . . . over my old letters. I cannot
tell you how it troubles me—and has from the first. I cannot 'see my
way clear' as the Friends say to accept pay for what I am no more the
author of than if I had never written the letters. An 'article' must be
composed like a picture out of sketches. The composition is not mine
and it is not right that I should be paid for a single sentence more than
the original fragment I sent you last spring. So there!!!"

6. "A California Mining Camp," *Scribner's Monthly* 15 (February
1878): 488-89. Cf. Foote's sketch with an earlier article on New
Almaden by J. Ross Browne, "Down in the Cinnabar Mines: A Visit to
New Almaden in 1865," *Harper's Monthly* 31 (October 1865): 345-56.

7. Gilder, *Book Buyer*, p. 342.

8. MHF to HG, January 1878. Foote's previous quotation is from
Reminiscences, p. 145.

9. MHF to HG and RWG, September 29, 1877; December 10, 1877.

10. "A Sea-port on the Pacific," *Scribner's Monthly* 16 (August 1878): 460.

11. "How Mandy Went Rowing with the 'Cap'n,' " *St. Nicholas Magazine* 5 (May 1878): 453.

12. MHF to HG, January 1879.

13. *Reminiscences*, p. 155; see also p. 137.

14. "In Exile," *Atlantic Monthly* 48 (August-September 1881), collected in *In Exile, and Other Stories* (Boston and New York, 1894), pp. 17-18.

15. "Introductory," *The Last Assembly Ball* (Boston and New York, 1889), p. 1.

16. Wallace Stegner, *Angle of Repose* (New York, 1971), pp. 61-62.

17. The illustrations for Holland's story appear in *Scribner's Monthly* 16 (August 1878): 529, 533, 536; the Burroughs "Bee" drawings can be found in *Scribner's Monthly* 18 (May 1879): 13, 14, 16; the "River" series appears in *Scribner's Monthly* 20 (August 1880): 482 passim. The literary works set in New Almaden are "A 'Muchacho' of the Mexican Camp," *St. Nicholas Magazine* 6 (December 1878): 79-81, and "The Cascarone Ball," *Scribner's Monthly* 18 (August 1879): 614-17.

18. *Reminiscences*, p. 189.

19. "Friend Barton's 'Concern,' " *Scribner's Monthly* 18 (July 1879), collected in *In Exile*, p. 121.

20. *Reminiscences*, p. 104.

21. Ibid., p. 166.

22. "A Story of the Dry Season," *Scribner's Monthly* 18 (September 1879): 778.

23. MHF to HG, spring 1882. Though this is a letter Foote wrote while revising *The Led-Horse Claim*, it is characteristic of her early epistolary descriptions of Leadville. For an interesting illustrated account of life in Leadville during this period see Ernest Ingersoll, "The Camp of the Carbonates: Ups and Downs in Leadville," *Scribner's Monthly* 18 (October 1879): 801-24. MHF contributed six of the illustrations.

24. Don L. and Jean H. Griswold, *The Carbonate Camp Called Leadville* (Denver, 1951), p. 238.

25. Levette Jay Davidson, "Letters from Authors," *Colorado Magazine* 19 (July 1942): 123. Griswold, *Carbonate Camp*, p. 249, reports MHF's descent into one of the mines Arthur managed; the incident was later transformed into fiction in *The Led-Horse Claim*.

26. MHF to Charles de Kay, July 8, 1879.

27. Helen Hunt Jackson's fiction, *Nelly's Silver Mine*, appeared in 1878. For MHF's account of her visit see *Reminiscences*, pp. 179-80, and Davidson, "Letters," p. 123.

28. Donaldson's description of Foote is reprinted from *Idaho of Yesterday* (Caldwell, Idaho, 1941), pp. 359-60.

29. The entry from Morse's manuscript diary (March 16, 1884) is quoted in *Reminiscences,* p. 23n.

30. MHF to HG, summer 1880.

31. *Reminiscences,* p. 196; see also p. 203.

32. The illustrations mentioned appear in the following: Owen Meredith, *Lucile* (Boston, 1881), passim; Ernest Ingersoll, "The Camp of the Carbonates," *Scribner's Monthly* 18 (October 1879): 803 passim; *Aucassin and Nicollette* (Ford, Howard, and Hulbert, 1880), passim; and Alfred Tennyson, *A Dream of Fair Women* (Boston, 1880), p. 99.

33. Armstrong, *Critic,* p. 135.

34. *Reminiscences,* pp. 211, 207.

35. See MHF to HG, August 14, 1881, for an account of MHF's exploration of an old hulk named the *Alquisar,* anchored in Penobscot Bay. The *Mary Spofford* of Foote's tale is probably derived from the *Mary Powell,* the boat on which MHF traveled between New York City and Milton.

36. "The Story of the Alcázar," *Century Magazine* 24 (June 1882), collected in *In Exile,* p. 143.

37. MHF to James Hague, January 30, 1883 (courtesy of the Henry E. Huntington Library).

38. R. W. Gilder's remarks are quoted in James Hart, *The Popular Book* (Berkeley and Los Angeles, 1963), p. 186. MHF is quoted in Davidson, "Letters," p. 123.

39. *The Led-Horse Claim: A Romance of a Mining Camp* (Boston, 1883), pp. 21–22.

40. MHF to James Hague, May 27, 1882 (courtesy of the Henry E. Huntington Library).

41. *Reminiscences,* p. 204.

42. MHF to HG, spring 1882.

43. *Reminiscences,* p. 205.

44. The letter to Hague is dated May 27, 1882 (courtesy of the Henry E. Huntington Library). MHF to HG, November 19, 1882.

45. *Reminiscences,* p. 102.

46. Ibid., pp. 265–66.

47. Ibid., p. 267.

48. Ibid., p. 273.

Chapter Three

1. See Paul, "Introduction" to *Reminiscences,* pp. 21–22. For a detailed account of the scheme see Paul L. Murphy, "Early Irrigation in the Boise Valley," *Pacific Northwest Quarterly* 44 (October 1953): 179–81.

2. MHF to RWG, December 12, 1883.

3. *John Bodewin's Testimony* (Boston, 1886), p. 193.

4. MHF to HG, June 17, 1884.

5. Foote, recognizing the necessity to "enforce [the] allusion and explanation of Bodewin's action—or want of action" (MHF to HG, September 18, 1884), provides him with a history of passivity. She develops his family background at length, emphasizing his loss of father and elder brother; his close relationship with his Quaker mother and younger sister; and his early inability to act resolutely, even when such indecisiveness insured that his sister would made a fateful marriage.

6. MHF to HG, April 1886.

7. Henry Nash Smith, *Virgin Land* (Cambridge, Mass., 1950), p. 229.

8. Bret Harte, "General Introduction" [1897], *The Luck of Roaring Camp and Other Tales* (Boston and New York, 1906), p. xvii.

9. A sketch by MHF of the "Stone House" appears in "An Idaho Picnic," *St. Nicholas Magazine* 14 (August 1887): 729–39; see also the photograph in *Reminiscences*, p. 27.

10. *Reminiscences*, p. 290.

11. "A Cloud on the Mountain," *Century Magazine* 31 (November 1885), collected in *In Exile*, p. 150.

12. V. L. Parrington, quoted in G. Harrison Orians, *A Short History of American Literature* (New York, 1940), p. 251.

13. All of MHF's comments to HG occur in a letter dated April 4, 1886.

14. MHF to HG, June 11, 1886.

15. "The Fate of a Voice," *Century Magazine* 33 (November 1886), collected in *The Last Assembly Ball* (Boston and New York, 1889), p. 218.

16. Cf. James's *Roderick Hudson* (1875), in which the hero finds love and art incompatible; the climactic coliseum scene adumbrates Foote's cliff scene. Cather's *The Song of the Lark* (1914), as the story of a gifted female singer, shares with Foote's story the use of the Lorelei motif and the cliff scene at Panther Canyon. For Foote's favorable comments on *The Song of the Lark*, see note 16 to Chapter 6, below.

17. MHF to HG, February 5, 1888.

18. MHF to HG, August 8, 1889.

19. MHF to HG, February 5, 1888.

20. MHF to HG, June 2, 1891; January 25, 1887; August 8, 1889; April 10, 1887.

21. "Pictures of the Far West" ["The Winter Camp—A Day's Ride from the Mail"], *Century Magazine* 39 (November 1889): 56.

22. Robert Taft, *Artists and Illustrators of the Old West, 1850–1900* (New York, 1953), p. 173.

23. MHF to RWG, February 3, 1888. The series appeared in *Century Magazine* 37–39 (November 1888–March 1889; May–August 1889;

October-November 1889): 108, 162, 449, 502, 687; 2, 299, 342, 502; 872, 57.

24. MHF to HG, June 6-8, 1887.
25. William Allen Rogers, *A World Worth While: A Record of 'Auld Acquaintance'* (New York, 1922), p. 188.
26. MHF to HG, May 28, 1879.
27. MHF to HG, April 10, 1887.
28. *The Last Assembly Ball* (Boston and New York, 1889), p. 12.
29. Smith, *Virgin Land*, p. 229.
30. Although MHF did not desire the "Pseudo-Romance" subtitle (see her letter of December 29, 1888, to RWG), her comments to Helena (summer 1887) suggest a philosophical basis for her choice, for the third time in a row, of the romance form.
31. MHF to HG, April 12, 1889.
32. MHF to HG, August 8, 1889. The quotation from *Reminiscences* appears on p. 311; see also Paul's "Introduction," pp. 31-35.
33. MHF to HG, January 8, 1888. Foote's previous quotation is from *Reminiscences,* p. 325.
34. *Reminiscences,* p. 329.
35. MHF to HG, February 22, 1888. See also her letter to Helena of July 18, 1891.
36. "The Rapture of Hetty," *Century Magazine* 43 (December 1891), collected in *In Exile,* p. 207.
37. The Henry E. Huntington Library's manuscript of "The Rapture of Hetty" reveals a lame conclusion which Foote decided against. The draft ends with supposition as to what Hetty's father said the next day, as to whether Basset had been wronged originally, and as to whether Hetty's father is anxious to seek vengeance or to smooth over the past.
38. MHF to RWG, December 8, 1891.

Chapter Four

1. MHF to HG, March 3-7, 1892.
2. *Reminiscences,* pp. 344-46.
3. MHF to Robert Underwood Johnson, April 19, 1891 (courtesy of the Henry E. Huntington Library). At this time the Indian Creek swindle probably had not occurred. While Foote seems to suggest in her *Reminiscences* that the episode took place during the summer and fall of 1892—*after The Chosen Valley* had appeared in serial form—it seems more probable from her letters, and from the uncanny correspondence between life and fiction here, that the incident occurred prior to the novel's completion.
4. MHF to HG, February 20, 1893.
5. *The Chosen Valley* (Boston and New York, 1892), pp. 17-18.

6. Armstrong, *Critic*, pp. 136–37.

7. See *Reminiscences*, pp. 376–78. See also Arthur Foote's own comments in T. A. Rickard, *Interviews with Mining Engineers* (San Francisco, 1922), p. 177, and Murphy, "Early Irrigation," pp. 179–81.

8. MHF to RWG, undated [c. February 1892].

9. W. D. Howells, "Editor's Study," *Harper's Monthly* 83 (November 1891): 963, and "Editor's Easy Chair," *Harper's Monthly* 124 (March 1912): 636–37.

10. Hamlin Garland, *Crumbling Idols* (Cambridge, Mass., rpt. 1960), pp. 52–54.

11. MHF to Mary Hague, September 26, 1893 (courtesy of the Henry E. Huntington Library).

12. Arthur's bouts with drinking decreased in frequency but continued to recur well into the twentieth century. As late as 1914, Mary was reporting to Helena periods of "the secret dread," as in her letter dated November 15: "I—if I may say it in your sacred ear of friendship—never feel safe to have him take journeys without me. A great trial in my life lifts and seems to pass away for long periods. Yet I am never free from the secret dread, and the risk to him, of these repeated fatal experiments—at long intervals—perhaps a whole year— increases with each one. The last took almost the form of a 'stroke.' This is very shattering—or undermining—to my old nerves. . . . I am a damaged piece of furniture, upholster myself as I may. . . . The last 'experiment' was last spring. . . ."

13. MHF to HG, September 1893. See also *Reminiscences*, pp. 354–57.

14. Cody, "Artist-Authors," p. 911. Foote's two illustrations for the series appeared in *Century Magazine* 46 (June-July 1893): 236, 392.

15. Charles Wolcott Balestier (1861-91) admired Foote's novels, especially *John Bodewin's Testimony*, about which he wrote to her. MHF reported to RWG, May 12, 1891, "Mr. Balestier gave me more pleasure and encouragement by his criticism on John Bodewin than anyone not you and Helena." *Benefits Forgot* (1892) bears a resemblance to *John Bodewin's Testimony* in its Colorado setting (Sangre de Cristo) and in the self-imposed plight of the sensitive hero, James Deed.

16. *Reminiscences*, p. 336. For details of the Footes' precarious finances see MHF to Mary Hague, January 12, 1893 (Henry E. Huntington Library) and MHF to HG, January 1895.

17. MHF to HG, November 11, 1892.

18. MHF to RWG, December 8, 1891.

19. "The Watchman," *Century Magazine* 47 (November 1893), collected in *In Exile*, pp. 241–42.

20. MHF to C. C. Buel, undated [c. late 1892] (courtesy of the

Henry E. Huntington Library). The previous quotation is from her letter to HG dated April 8, 1887.

21. MHF to C. C. Buel, undated [c. late 1892] (courtesy of the Henry E. Huntington Library).

22. Robert Wayne Smith, "The Coeur d'Alene Mining War of 1892," *Oregon State Monographs: Studies in History,* #2 (Corvallis, Ore., 1961), p. 15. See also the early article by George Edgar French, "The Coeur d'Alene Riots, 1892," *Overland Monthly* 26 (July 1895): 32-49.

23. Smith, "Mining War," p. 30.

24. Weldon B. Heyburn, later U.S. senator from Idaho, was named principal legal counsel for the MOA in 1891 and directed the prosecution of the miners' union in state and federal courts. Termed "the broadest and by far, to my thinking, the cleverest man in Idaho" by MHF, Heyburn provided his author friend with factual memoranda for the novel. See MHF's note and letter to C. C. Buel, undated [c. late 1892] (Henry E. Huntington Library).

25. Unsigned review, "Literature," *Critic* 25 (November 17, 1894): 327.

26. MHF to C. C. Buel, undated [c. late 1892] (courtesy of the Henry E. Huntington Library).

27. *Coeur d'Alene* (Boston and New York, 1894), p. 46.

28. For information on the subsequent interest in *Coeur d'Alene* see MHF to RWG, June 4, 1896, and James H. Maguire, *Mary Hallock Foote* (Boise, 1972), pp. 19–20.

29. MHF to C. C. Buel, undated [c. late 1892] (courtesy of the Henry E. Huntington Library).

30. *The Chosen Valley,* p. 186.

31. The story may have evolved from the "Section No. 13" idea Foote abandoned in 1886 (see letter to HG, November 1, 1886). At any rate it was completed by February 1892. See her letter to HG, February 15, 1892, for the background of the story: "The setting was bored into me on our last journey West when we were snow-bound on the Oregon short-line for two days."

32. "On a Side-Track," *The Cup of Trembling, and Other Stories* (Boston and New York, 1895), p. 121. Page references for all four of the collected stories are to this volume.

33. See Donald L. McMurry, *Coxey's Army* (Seattle, 1968), p. 215, for a brief note on the Boise situation.

34. MHF to RWG, January 15, 1894 (courtesy of the Henry E. Huntington Library).

35. Unsigned review, "Recent Fiction," *Nation* 62 (February 27, 1896): 182.

36. *Reminiscences,* p. 269.

37. Ibid., p. 395.

Chapter Five

1. *Reminiscences*, p. 309. The previous quotation is from MHF to HG, May 8, 1896. Betty Foote's publications included "The Youngest," *Atlantic Monthly* 92 (July 1903); "The Inter-veil," *Century Magazine*, 67 (March 1904); "A Girl of the Engineers," *Atlantic Monthly*, 95 (March 1905); "The Music-Makers," *Atlantic Monthly* 98 (July 1906); and "The Laboratory in the Hills," *Atlantic Monthly* 98 (December 1906).

2. Winthrop S. Scudder to MHF, February 9, 1900.

3. Joseph Pennell, *The Adventures of an Illustrator* (Boston, 1925), p. 58. Abbey is quoted in Armstrong, *Critic*, p. 132.

4. Armstrong, *Critic*, pp. 131, 141.

5. See MHF to HG, January 3, 1898: "I haven't been long enough in Grass Valley to get outside of Grass Valley." In the years following MHF seems to have written only one other short story with a Grass Valley setting. Titled "On Trust" and never published, it was written after the outbreak of World War I; a typescript is at Stanford University Library.

6. Wallace Stegner, *Selected American Prose*, p. 118. Stegner, pp. 117–19, reprints passages from MHF's letters to HG of October 16, 1896, and February 7, 1897.

7. "How the Pump Stopped at the Morning Watch," *Century Magazine* 58 (July 1899): 470.

8. Bret Harte, "The Rise of the 'Short Story,' " *Cornhill* 7 (July 1899): 8.

9. MHF to HG, December 22, 1897.

10. For details of this trip, see Rodman Paul's prefatory comments to his excerpting of "The Harshaw Bride" in *Idaho Yesterdays* 20 (Summer 1976): 18-32. The germ of the story may have come from the instance of the transatlantic engagement MHF alludes to in *Reminiscences*, p. 121. Though Foote notes in her autobiography that the tale was written when her "fortunes were far from gay," her mood and prospects were much improved by the time she submitted it in October 1895.

11. See Paul, *Idaho Yesterdays*, p. 18n. Pilgrim Station was a stage stop on the route to Thousand Springs. When published in the 1903 volume *A Touch of Sun and Other Stories*, "Pilgrim Station" was retitled "The Maid's Progress" in order to avoid confusion with "Pilgrims to Mecca," another story in the collection.

12. *Reminiscences*, p. 121. Foote's older daughter Betty attended eastern schools as did Agnes for one year; in neither case did Foote move East with them. But see MHF to HG, April 3, 1891.

13. In Browning's play, Merton himself is the earlier lover of Mildred, so the latter has always been "true" to him, while Foote's

story stresses that Helen's escapade did not have irreversible consequences, that she is still "pure."

14. Unsigned review, *Seattle Times,* December 27, 1903.

15. Charles F. Lummis, "The New League for Literature and the West," *Land of Sunshine* 8 (April 1898): 208.

16. Charles F. Lummis, "That Which Is Written," *Land of Sunshine* 14 (February 1901): 157.

17. *The Prodigal* (Boston and New York, 1900), p. 1.

18. MHF to HG, November 22, 1900.

19. Charles F. Lummis, "That Which Is Written," *Land of Sunshine* 14 (February 1901): 157. See also unsigned review, "Books of the Week," *Outlook* 66 (December 1, 1900): 856.

20. *The Wrecker* is a collaboration by Stevenson and his stepson, Lloyd Osbourne. An unsigned review of *The Prodigal,* "Books of the Week," *Outlook* 66 (December 1, 1900): 856, states, "There is a certain direct vigor of character-sketching here that reminds one of Stevenson." An incidental similarity between *The Prodigal* and Stevenson's *The Wrecker* is the use of a "remittance man." While Clunie Robert receives 50 cents a day from a partner of the shipping firm, Norris Carthew is offered one shilling a day in Australia by his father's lawyer.

21. *The Desert and the Sown* (Boston and New York, 1902), pp. 133-34.

22. MHF to HG, December 15, 1901. See also MHF to RWG, August 26, 1901.

23. Bliss Perry to MHF, December 5, 1901.

24. MHF to HG, May 18, 1904.

25. Janet Foote Micoleau to Mary Lou Benn, July 18, 1955, quoted in Benn, *Colorado Magazine,* p. 108.

26. MHF gave generously of her time and talent to the hospital for several years and donated to it all the profits of her collected juvenile tales, *The Little Fig-Tree Stories* (1899).

27. MHF to the Knickerbocker Publishing Company, December 2, 1905 (courtesy of the State Historical Society of Wisconsin). Foote's uncollected tale "The Eleventh Hour," which appeared in *Century Magazine* in January 1906, had been written and submitted before Agnes's death.

28. "Gideon's Knock," *The Spinners' Book of Fiction* (San Francisco, 1907), p. 86.

29. MHF to HG, January 19, 1911. See *Reminiscences,* p. 384, and MHF to Robert Underwood Johnson, April 15, 1896 (the Henry E. Huntington Library) for details of the one earlier rejection of a Foote manuscript by Johnson, associate editor of *Century Magazine.*

30. MHF to HG, October 25, 1915.

31. MHF to HG, January 19, 1911.

32. Orians, *Short History,* p.251

33. Cecil Williams, Avowal Scenes in American Historical Fiction: A Study of Fin de Siècle Literary Taste," *Bulletin of Oklahoma State University* 48, Humanities Series #2 (September 30, 1951): 29.

34. *The Royal Americans* (Boston and New York, 1910), p. 385.

35. *A Picked Company* (Boston and New York, 1912), p. 405.

36. MHF to HG, April 30, 1893.

Chapter Six

1. MHF to HG, September 23, 1915. See also MHF to HG, January 27, 1915.

2. *The Valley Road* (Boston and New York, 1915), p. 286.

3. MHF to HG, September 23, 1915. The opening stanzas of "The Valley Road" might be construed to bear upon the fictional situation of *The Valley Road,* but the poem in its entirety militates against such an interpretation.

4. MHF also patterned the Torresville engineering scheme in part on a successful hydraulic mining project in which her husband had participated. See Arthur's article, "The Redemption of the Great Valley of California," *Transactions of the American Society of Civil Engineers* 35 (September 1909): 830-46.

5. Unsigned review, "Current Fiction," *Nation* 101 (December 30, 1915): 778.

6. MHF to HG, undated letter [postmarked April 7, 1913].

7. The germ for this situation probably derives from Helena Gilder's proposal more than thirty years earlier that MHF's unmarried sister Philadelphia join the Gilder household as a companion-governess. MHF, pleased at the idea, had written Helena in July 1882: "It is almost as great a 'compliment' to pay a woman as asking her to marry you—to ask her to come and live in your house and take the initiative in your child's education."

8. MHF to HG, undated [c. summer 1892].

9. *Edith Bonham* (Boston and New York, 1919), p. 326.

10. MHF to HG, October 1, 1874.

11. *The Ground-Swell* (Boston and New York: Houghton Mifflin Company, 1919), p. 134.

12. James Hague's son Billy died in France in 1918 from pneumonia. The quoted passage from the novel's conclusion anticipates MHF's final paragraphs in *Reminiscences;* see p. 152 above.

13. MHF to HG, August 1, 1915.

14. Davidson, "Letters," p. 123.

15. MHF to Edward S. Holden, March 28, 1894 (courtesy of the Lick Archives, University of California, Santa Cruz).

16. See MHF to HG, April 23, 1916, on *The Song of the Lark:* "It is a fine, fresh, vital thing. So much better than one could expect. . . . All

stories of genius make one shake one's head in doubt. This one is as real
as genius itself, and she has a great grip on that country—the author."
See her letter of February 7, 1912, to HG on the work of Sedgwick.

17. Eric Howard, "Famous Californians: Mary Hallock Foote," *San
Francisco Call,* April 3, 1923, [p. 7].

18. The fragment "Backgrounds with Figures" was returned from
Commonweal in January 1930. See Paul's explanation, *Reminiscences,*
pp. xi-xii, of the genesis and dating of the published version.

19. *Reminiscences,* p. 400. Foote's comment to Helena is from an
undated letter [1894].

20. There is no evidence that Foote ever corresponded with Twain.
Benjamin De Casseres's publication, in *When Huck Finn Went
Highbrow* (New York, 1934), of an 1887 Twain letter purported to be to
MHF is in fact to an unidentified older woman of the same surname.

21. Consider, for example, Susan Magoffin's *Down the Santa Fe Trail
and Into Mexico* (New Haven, 1926), the diary of a bride's trip West in
1846; Flora Cloman's *I'd Live It Over* (New York, 1941), the
autobiography of a woman who spent her early life in western mining
camps; and the letters of Louise Amelia Knapp Smith Clapp (1819-
1906) which describe the California gold rush.

22. Caroline M. Kirkland, "Preface" [1839], *A New Home—Who'll
Follow?* (New York, 1850), pp. 3-4.

23. Arthur De Wint Foote died August 24, 1933. For an assessment
of his professional accomplishments see the published account by his
son, "Arthur DeWint [*sic*] Foote," *Transactions of the American
Society of Civil Engineers* 99 (1934): 1449-52. See also the tribute by
D. W. Ross in *Boise Idaho Statesmen* (February 24, 1909), reprinted in
Reminiscences, pp. 377-78, and Arthur's own comments in T. A.
Rickard, *Interviews with Mining Engineers* (San Francisco, 1922), pp.
171-89.

24. At her request, Mary Hallock Foote was buried in the West—at
Grass Valley, California.

25. Edmund Kinyon, "Early Leaving of Mr. and Mrs. Arthur D. Foote
is Occasion for Regrets Among Grass Valley People," *Grass Valley-
Nevada City Union,* June 5, 1932, p. 3, quoted in *Reminiscences,* p. 44.
Mrs. Micoleau's remarks appear in Benn, *Colorado Magazine,* p. 108.

Chapter Seven

1. *The Last Assembly Ball,* p.1.
2. Owen Wister, *Members of the Family* (New York, 1911), p. 15.
3. Gilder, *Book Buyer,* p. 342.

Selected Bibliography

PRIMARY SOURCES

1. Books (in chronological order)

The Led-Horse Claim: A Romance of a Mining Camp. Boston: James R. Osgood and Company, 1883.
John Bodewin's Testimony. Boston: Ticknor and Company, 1886.
The Last Assembly Ball: A Pseudo Romance of the Far West. Boston and New York: Houghton, Mifflin and Company, 1889. ("The Fate of a Voice.")
The Chosen Valley. Boston and New York: Houghton, Mifflin and Company, 1892.
Coeur d'Alene. Boston and New York: Houghton, Mifflin and Company, 1894.
In Exile, and Other Stories. Boston and New York: Houghton, Mifflin and Company, 1894. ("In Exile," "Friend Barton's 'Concern,'" "The Story of the Alcázar," "The Rapture of Hetty," and "The Watchman.")
The Cup of Trembling, and Other Stories. Boston and New York: Houghton, Mifflin and Company, 1895. ("The Cup of Trembling," "Maverick," "On a Side-Track," and "The Trumpeter.")
The Little Fig-Tree Stories. Boston and New York: Houghton, Mifflin and Company, 1899. ("Flower of the Almond," "The Lamb That Couldn't Keep Up," "Dream Horses," "An Idaho Picnic," "A Visit to John's Camp," "November in the Cañon," "The Gates on Grandfather's Farm," "The Garrett at Grandfather's," and "The Spare Bedroom at Grandfather's.")
The Prodigal. Boston and New York: Houghton, Mifflin and Company, 1900.
The Desert and the Sown. Boston and New York: Houghton Mifflin Company, 1902.
A Touch of Sun and Other Stories. Boston and New York: Houghton Mifflin Company, 1903. ("A Touch of Sun," "The Maid's Progress," "Pilgrims to Mecca," and "The Harshaw Bride.")
The Royal Americans. Boston and New York: Houghton Mifflin Company, 1910.

A Picked Company. Boston and New York: Houghton Mifflin Company, 1912.
The Valley Road. Boston and New York: Houghton Mifflin Company, 1915.
Edith Bonham. Boston and New York: Houghton Mifflin Company, 1917.
The Ground-Swell. Boston and New York: Houghton Mifflin Company, 1919.
A Victorian Gentlewoman in the Far West: The Reminiscences of Mary Hallock Foote. Ed. Rodman W. Paul. San Marino, Calif.: The Huntington Library, 1972.

2. Uncollected Materials (in chronological order)

"The Picture in the Fire-place Bedroom." *St. Nicholas Magazine* 2 (February 1875): 248-50.
"A California Mining Camp." *Scribner's Monthly* 15 (February 1878): 480-93.
"How Mandy Went Rowing with the 'Cap'n.' " *St. Nicholas Magazine* 5 (May 1878): 449-53.
"A Sea-port on the Pacific." *Scribner's Monthly* 16 (August 1878): 449-60.
"A 'Muchacho' of the Mexican Camp." *St. Nicholas Magazine* 6 (December 1878): 79-81.
"The Cascarone Ball." *Scribner's Monthly* 18 (August 1879): 614-17.
"A Story of the Dry Season." *Scribner's Monthly* 18 (September 1879): 766-81.
"The Children's 'Claim.' " *St. Nicholas Magazine* 7 (January 1880): 238-45.
"Cousin Charley's Story." *St. Nicholas Magazine* 8 (February 1881): 271-76.
"A Diligence Journey in Mexico." *Century Magazine* 23 (November 1881): 1-14.
"A Provincial Capital of Mexico." *Century Magazine* 23 (January 1882): 321-33.
"From Morelia to Mexico City on Horseback." *Century Magazine* 23 (March 1882): 643-55.
"Menhaden Sketches: Summer at Christmas-Time." *St. Nicholas Magazine* 12 (December 1884): 116-24.
"Pictures of the Far West." *Century Magazine* 37-39 (November 1888-November 1889), passim.
"A Four-Leaved Clover in the Desert." *St. Nicholas Magazine* 21 (May-June 1894), 644-50; 694-99.

"The Borrowed Shift." *Land of Sunshine* 10 (December 1898), 13–24.
"How the Pump Stopped at the Morning Watch." *Century Magazine* 58 (July 1899), 469–72.
"The Eleventh Hour." *Century Magazine* 71 (January 1906), 485–93.
"Gideon's Knock." *The Spinners' Book of Fiction* (San Francisco: Paul Elder and Company, 1907), 77–91.

3. Unpublished Materials

"On Trust." Typescript short story. Stanford University Library, Stanford, California.

Three autobiographical fragments. Stanford University Library.

Approximately 540 letters, primarily to Helena de Kay Gilder. Stanford University Library. Copies of these letters are at the Henry E. Huntington Library, San Marino, California, and the Bancroft Library, University of California, Berkeley.
Approximately 45 letters, primarily to James Hague, as well as 30 letters to *Century Magazine*. The Henry E. Huntington Library.
Small collections of letters at New York Public Library; Library of Congress; National Portrait Gallery, Washington; Humanities Research Center, University of Texas; State Historical Society of Wisconsin; Beinecke Library, Yale University; and Widener Library, Harvard University.

SECONDARY SOURCES

"The American Personality: The Artist-Illustrator of Life in the United States, 1860-1930." Grunwald Center for the Graphic Arts Exhibition Catalogue (Los Angeles: UCLA, 1976). A collection of useful essays on turn-of-the-century illustration. Features two of MHF's drawings and numerous references to her work.
ARMSTRONG, REGINA. "Representative American Women Illustrators." *Critic* 37 (August 1900): 131-41. A sympathetic analysis of MHF as a female artist.
BENN, MARY LOU. "Mary Hallock Foote: Early Leadville Writer." *Colorado Magazine* 33 (April 1956): 93-108. Benn's two introductory articles are drawn from her unpublished Master's thesis, "Mary Hallock Foote: Pioneer Woman Novelist" (University of Wyoming, 1955).
———. "Mary Hallock Foote in Idaho." *University of Wyoming Publications* 20 (July 15, 1956): 157-78. This special issue contains other essays on MHF.

Cody, Alpheus Sherwin. "Artist-Authors." *Outlook* 49 (May 26, 1894), 910-11. Brief discussion of MHF, Howard Pyle, and George Du Maurier.

Davidson, Levette Jay. "Letters from Authors." *Colorado Magazine* 19 (July 1942): 122-25. Publication of two letters written by MHF during October 1922.

Donaldson, Thomas. *Idaho of Yesterday.* Caldwell, Idaho: Caxton Printers, Ltd., 1941. 358-63. Includes interesting description of MHF in Leadville, Colorado.

Etulain, Richard W. "Mary Hallock Foote (1847-1938)." *American Literary Realism, 1870-1910,* 5 (Spring 1972): 145-50.

———. "Mary Hallock Foote: A Checklist." *Western American Literature* 10 (May 1975): 59-65. A listing of MHF's writings by categories; also includes secondary materials.

Foote, Arthur B. "Memoir of Arthur DeWint [sic] Foote." *Transactions of the American Society of Civil Engineers* 99 (1934): 1449-52. A valuable estimate of Arthur Foote's professional accomplishments by his son.

Gilder, Helena de Kay. "Author Illustrators, II: Mary Hallock Foote." *Book Buyer* 11 (August 1894): 338-42. A charming tribute by Foote's best friend.

Griswold, Don L. and Jean H. *The Carbonate Camp Called Leadville.* Denver: University of Denver Press, 1951.

Hart, James D. *The Popular Book: A History of America's Literary Taste.* Berkeley and Los Angeles: University of California Press, rpt. 1963.

Linton, W. J. "The History of Wood-Engraving in America: Part IV," *American Art and American Art Collections.* Ed. Walter Montgomery. Boston, 1889. I, 464-70. Includes two MHF illustrations and a brief tribute by her mentor-teacher.

Lummis, Charles F. "The New League for Literature and the West." *Land of Sunshine* 8 (April 1898): 206-09.

Maguire, James H. *Mary Hallock Foote.* Boise: Boise State College, 1972. A pamphlet in the Western Writers series; provides a useful overview of Foote's fiction.

Paul, Rodman W. *Mining Frontiers of the Far West, 1848-1880.* New York, 1963.

———. "When Culture Came to Boise: Mary Hallock Foote in Idaho." *Idaho Yesterdays* 20 (Summer 1976): 2-12. An extremely knowledgeable essay on MHF's years in Idaho by the editor of her autobiography. The issue is dedicated to Foote-related materials.

Rogers, W. A. *A World Worth While: A Record of 'Auld Acquaintance.'* New York: Harper and Brothers, 1922. 183-88. Brief discussion of MHF by one of her distinguished contemporaries.

SPENCE, CLARK C. *Mining Engineers and the American West: The Lace-Boot Brigade, 1849-1933*. New Haven: Yale University Press, 1970.

STEGNER, WALLACE. *Angle of Repose*. New York: Doubleday & Company, 1971. MHF serves as the model for the fictional heroine of this Pulitzer-Prize winning novel, which was adapted into opera in 1976.

TAFT, ROBERT. *Artists and Illustrators of the Old West: 1850-1900*. New York: Charles Scribner's Sons, 1953. An evaluative discussion of MHF which pairs her with William Allen Rogers; reprint of an earlier article.

Index